THE TASMANIA STORY

by

LLOYD ROBSON

OXFORD
UNIVERSITY PRESS

Melbourne

OXFORD UNIVERSITY PRESS AUSTRALIA

OXFORD   NEW YORK   TORONTO
DELHI   BOMBAY   CALCUTTA   MADRAS   KARACHI
PETALING JAYA   SINGAPORE   HONG KONG   TOKYO
NAIROBI   DAR ES SALAAM   CAPE TOWN
MELBOURNE   AUCKLAND
and associated companies in BERLIN   IBADAN

OXFORD is a trademark of Oxford University Press

First published 1987
Reprinted in 1988

National Library of Australia
Cataloguing-in-Publication data:

Robson, L.L. (Leslie Lloyd), 1931–
   The Tasmanian story.

   Includes index.
   ISBN 0 19 554778 0.

   1. Tasmania — History. I. Title.

994.6

Designed by Jennifer Johnston
Typeset by Post Typesetters, Stones Corner, Qld
Printed by Brown Prior Anderson, Melbourne
Published by Oxford University Press,
253 Normanby Road, South Melbourne, Australia

Cover photograph: Lake Pedder, south-western
Tasmania, is reproduced by permission of the
Tasmanian Department of Tourism.

Contents

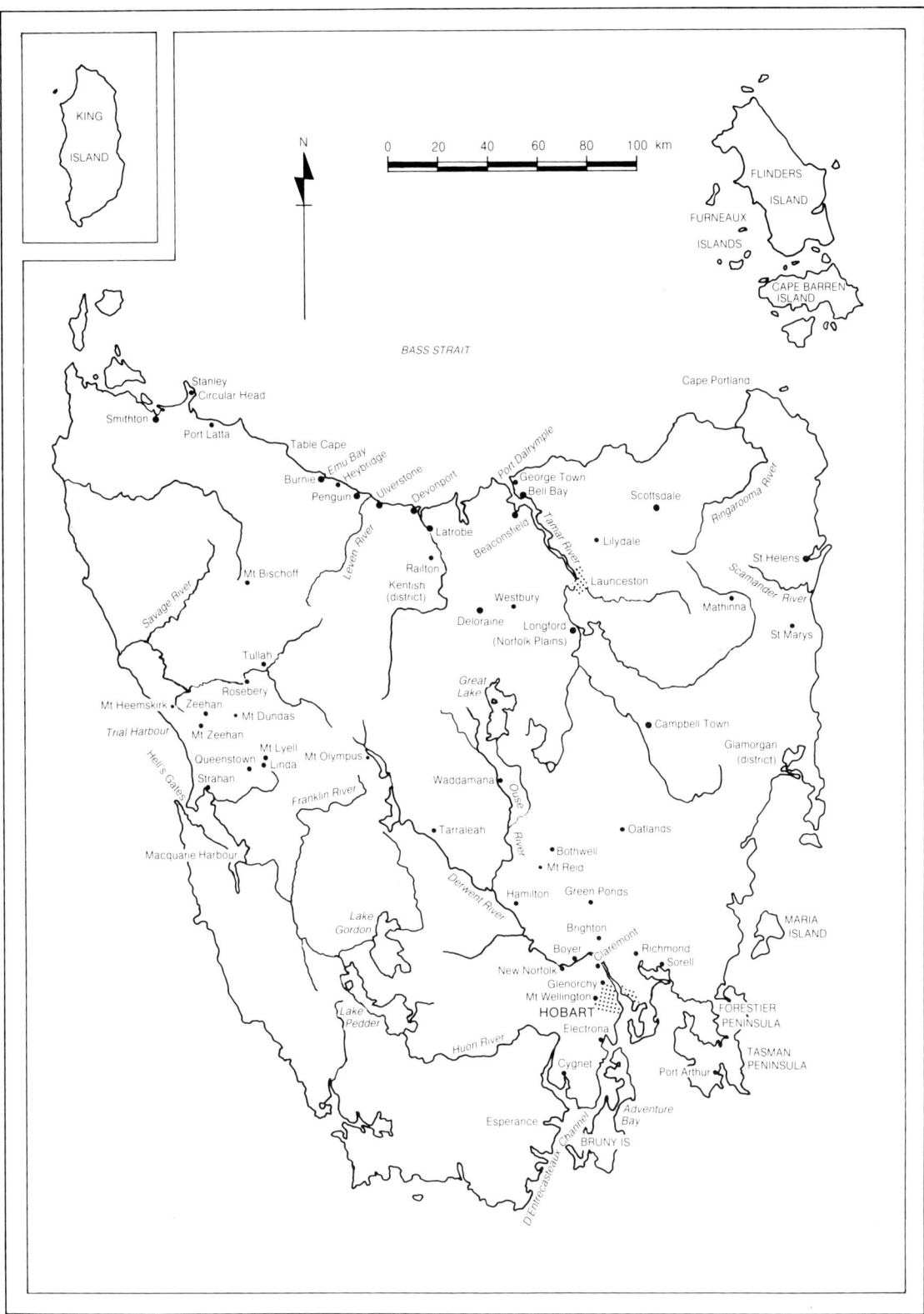

CHAPTER 1

Invasion

T HE PRESENT ISLAND OF TASMANIA was once part of the continent of Australia, forming a cape attached to the mainland. Then, about 18 000 years ago, the ice caps at the poles gradually began melting. The seas rose, and by about 12 000 years ago Tasmania had been cut off from mainland Australia.

The final link with Australia proper to be submerged was the area stretching from what is now known as Wilson's Promontory in Victoria through the Furneaux Islands, to the north-east tip of Tasmania. Flinders Island became separated from the mainland, King and Maria Islands were cut off from Tasmania, and finally the Flinders Island–Tasmania land connection was severed. Glaciers in the central and southern areas of the island also melted, forming numerous small lakes that are still to be seen in parts of the central highlands.

The Aborigines

It is unknown when human beings first occupied the area that Europeans named Van Diemen's Land. Recent research suggests that people were present at least 20 000 years ago and it is likely that they represent the southernmost human occupation of the world.

These people were nomadic and like other wanderers were preoccupied with hunting animals for food and gathering such items as berries and eggs to add to their diet.

The first recorded evidence of their physical appearance dates only from the late eighteenth century when French and English sea explorers visited the island. By then the Tasmanian Aborigines had probably developed their own distinctive physical characteristics as a result of their isolation from the Aborigines on the mainland.

These inhabitants of the island were seen as a people without fixed habitations, dark in skin colour and with distinctive frizzy hair. It is unknown exactly how many Aborigines there were before white settlement; figures based on rough estimates made by the Europeans after they occupied the island suggest that the Aboriginal population was between 4000 and 6000.

The culture of the Van Diemen's Land people was that of nomadic tribes, though it is possible that for some part of the year certain of them in the cold western region occupied sites of small 'villages'.

The Aborigines were a hunter-gatherer people and their island provided ample food. No crops were sown to be harvested and no animals were domesticated until the Europeans brought dogs. Spears, waddies (clubs) and snares (traps) were used to capture wallabies, kangaroos and small marsupials. With the aid of grass ropes, trees were scaled to capture possums.

Principal hunting weapons were the spear, brought to a sharp point by scraping with small worked stone implements, and the waddy. No implements with handles were used and neither was the boomerang nor the spear-thrower. In other words, the tool-kit was simple and suited to the environment.

Although water was never far away in Van Diemen's Land kelp was made into small buckets for carrying it. Baskets were also woven. Water was the only liquid drunk except occasionally for a form of cider-like drink produced from a particular type of gum tree.

Until a baffling change of diet about 4000 years ago, fish from the sea were also consumed. As there is no evidence of fish hooks being used, the fish were presumably caught by constructing traps made of rocks, so that at low tide the fish could be grabbed by hand or speared.

Made from large bundles of bark or rushes lashed together, these canoe–rafts seem to have been used only by Aborigines in the south and west of Van Diemen's Land. A thin pole, or perhaps a spear, was used to guide the canoe–raft through the water.

Mannalargenna was the highly intelligent chief of the Oyster Bay Aborigines who lived in the area between St Patrick's Head and the Schoutens. He accompanied G. A. Robinson to the Furneaux Islands, and died there in 1835. He was 173 cm tall, taller than most Europeans at that time.

Jinny, from the Port Sorell district, has the characteristic close-cropped hair style of Aboriginal women and decorative bands of kangaroo skin around her neck.

Crayfish and shellfish were also eaten, the women taking on the task of diving for or gathering these sources of food, which did not become taboo like scaled fish.

At certain times of the year, birds' eggs provided food, and seals too were captured, sometimes by the Aborigines crossing to off-shore islands in a form of canoe-raft made from bundles of bark lashed together. These craft, though wrongly, have been termed catamarans.

Meat was semi-cooked or grilled after being thrown on the open fire. There were no methods for stewing in pots and ovens were also unknown.

Visiting sea explorers reported the people of the island to be perfectly in harmony with their environment. The bush and undergrowth were continually burnt by the Aborigines to encourage fresh growth on which such animals as kangaroo and wallaby could feed and thereby become prey for the hunter. The fire-stick was generally carried and the Aborigines made a practice of setting fire to the bush as they walked along.

There is no evidence of the birth-rate but the family group was basic. It consisted of husband, wife and children and perhaps a few other close relatives. Families formed a loose-knit combination with each other, and clans seem to have been another larger unit. These in turn were linked within larger language-units.

There were at least five language units in the island. Whether these were developed from a common language is unknown, but the result was that group A could get an idea of what group B was saying and B could follow group C, but A could not understand C.

Boundaries were probably based on hunting areas or some natural division such as a river or chain of mountains. The mining of ochre was important enough for informal arrangements to be understood so that a group might pass through alien territory, perhaps at certain times of the year, for the purpose of extracting the ochre.

The ochre, consisting of clay and hydrated oxide of iron, was mined by the women using wooden chisels. It was prised out and, after being pounded, it was mixed with animal grease and used as a type of pomade or dressing for the hair. Many European observers remarked on the male Aborigines' reddened, mop-like heads of hair. Women wore their hair short, in the form of a crew-cut.

These original inhabitants of Van Diemen's Land believed that they and their island had originally been created by beings who moved in the sky, among the stars. Story-telling about this, together with tales of everyday events, was popular. Dances were performed by adults, and children indulged in games.

The main shelter was a form of wind-break, made by branches and limbs of trees thrown together temporarily. In front of this rough-and-ready shelter, fires were kindled by the fire-stick and the people prepared and ate their meals and slept on the bare ground.

There is no evidence that the Aboriginal people were able to create flame by using flints or other instruments. They took little fires on a clay base with them in their canoe-rafts when venturing to the off-shore islands.

These people were about 168 cm tall (men) and 153 cm (women), but there was a good deal of variation, as among all peoples. Many adults bore distinctive marks or cicatrices, formed by cutting the skin and inserting charcoal so that a raised scar was formed. These may have been to distinguish certain groups of people.

Personal adornments consisted of shell necklaces and a type of kangaroo-hide bangle, armulet or necklace. Lucky charms and pretty objects were also probably carried. Mostly the people went naked but women with babies had kangaroo-skin carrying bags on their backs.

If people were sick, sometimes little pouches containing the ashes of the dead were placed over the sore place. Broken legs or arms were straightened by splints tied with string made from strong grass, and doubtless potions were swallowed for some illnesses.

Cremation of the dead was practised and there is evidence of intriguing and elaborate burial structures, perhaps for people of distinction.

Unfortunately relatively little is known of Aboriginal culture in depth and much of our knowledge is derived from European observations made at a time when the black people were decimated and demoralized.

This cremation site on Maria Island is in the form of a four-sided pyramid, with the original structure of bark (left), partly opened (right) and the contents (centre). The ashes of the cremated Aborigine were covered with carefully arranged grass, and held down by twigs weighted with stones.

European Interest

The Dutch explorer Abel Tasman, who discovered and named Van Diemen's Land in 1642, had been instructed to search for trading opportunities and, when he found none, sailed on. Then in the late eighteenth century French and English voyagers touched at southern Van Diemen's Land during their reconnaissance of the Pacific. They charted parts of the coastline and generally established good relations with the Aborigines.

Adventure Bay on Bruny Island was a favoured anchorage for European maritime expeditions since it was sheltered and had good supplies of wood and water. In the following years European whalers and sealers became active in the waters off Van Diemen's Land but no permanent settlement was attempted until 1803.

Abel Janszoon Tasman (c. 1603–59), was employed by the Dutch East India Company when he sighted Van Diemen's Land on 24 November 1642, and named it in honour of the governor-general of the Company.

British Settlement

In that year Lieutenant John Bowen and a small party consisting mainly of convicts arrived in the Derwent from Sydney. P. G. King, the governor of New South Wales, had directed Bowen to form the settlement on the basis that the French were likely to occupy the southern part of the continent unless the British beat them to it.

At the same time the British government sent an expedition across the world to Port Phillip, again to forestall the French and nip their commercial ambitions in the bud. The British appointed David Collins as the Lieutenant-Governor of the proposed new settlement. On arrival Collins decided that Port Phillip would not suit as a harbour because the entrance was so treacherous. Lacking a plentiful supply of fresh water at Sorrento, where he established his camp, and troubled by the hot weather and indiscipline, he moved to the Derwent in 1804.

Meanwhile Governor King sent Lieutenant Colonel William Paterson to Port Dalrymple, again to establish a British presence and safeguard British interests. Sixteen years after the first fleet came to Sydney Cove, then, the British expanded their occupied territory to take in Van Diemen's Land.

It must be stressed that motives for settlement were essentially commercial. The necessary conditions for occupation were availability of a convict labour force and importantly a good safe harbour, reliable supplies of fresh water, and suitable soil for the sowing and harvesting of crops. It was optimistically hoped that the infant settlement would thereby become self-reliant.

The first European settlements on Van Diemen's Land were basically out-stations of New South Wales and governed from Sydney, which in turn was under orders from London. All these settlements were colonial creations of Britain and were formed to be of benefit to the colonizing country. From the beginning they were interlocked with Britain and perceived in terms of benefiting British interests.

Early Van Diemen's Land

Both the Derwent and Port Dalrymple settlements led a precarious existence, utterly dependent on supplies from Sydney, India or the Cape of Good Hope. Sometimes these sources failed to deliver and rationing became necessary. Food supplies were supplemented by meat from kangaroos and emus and, as time went on, from wheat crops.

Most of the newcomers were convicts and the settlements from the start depended on the muscle-power of this labour force for building and agriculture.

Another feature of the early settlements was the very large number of men to women. The few adult females were extremely vulnerable in such a violent society as Van Diemen's Land and had little choice but to become associated with a male protector.

Life was barbarous in these penal settlements. At home, the Napoleonic wars were raging and the British government paid little attention to the new possessions, apart from keeping up a supply of convicts.

During the early years of the Van Diemen's Land settlement population increased suddenly with the arrival of the Norfolk Islanders. They were freed convicts who had been originally sent from Sydney to Norfolk Island, and their origins were remembered in the names of New Norfolk and Norfolk Plains (later re-named Longford).

Van Diemen's Land remained under the control of Sydney. From there, Governor Macquarie visited Van Diemen's Land in 1811. He laid out and named the main streets of Hobart Town and on a journey to Launceston also named many areas in the hinterland.

In 1812 the settlements in the north and south were brought under one administration and the official capital of the colony was named as Hobart Town.

During these years large numbers of convicts escaped from the settlement and formed various bandit or bushranger gangs that roamed the interior, defying the forces of government and terrorizing the pioneer settlers. One of the most famous bushrangers was

Michael Howe, remembered especially as the subject of the first book published in Australia (in 1818 at Hobart Town).

The military stationed in the colony sought to defeat the menace of the bandits, who were eventually beaten by force of numbers and fire-power. Once this had been accomplished the soldiers were unleashed on the Aborigines.

After the end of the war with France, the British government encouraged free settlers to go out to Van Diemen's Land. These ambitious and often quite wealthy settlers took advantage of the system of free land grants and began occupying the excellent pastoral country between Hobart Town and Launceston, with spurs to the east and west.

Meanwhile wheat flourished at Norfolk Plains and in the Sorell-Richmond area. It yielded such excellent crops in the early stages that an export trade to New South Wales sprang up. As more and more of the land was settled and given over to cattle raising, and eventually to wool-growing, conflict with the Aborigines sharply increased. There ensued a life and death struggle for possession of the land.

Aborigines attacked workmen's huts and the colonists took bloody reprisals and launched violent attacks. Continual skirmishes occurred. The sudden appearance and then disappearance of war-like Aborigines frightened the settlers and convinced them that their enemy was numerous, determined and formidable.

This frontier war could have only one conclusion if English settlers continued to arrive, hungry for land. The Aborigines were few in number and, in comparison with the whites, poorly armed. Though resourceful and highly skilled in guerrilla or bandit warfare, they were hopelessly out-gunned and had little chance to regroup. Their culture was shattered and their population depleted. Responding to this terrible threat, in the early 1820s the black people brought their desperate resistance to its height in many attacks on the invaders.

Meanwhile the Lieutenant-Governor of Van Diemen's Land, David Collins, died suddenly in 1810. The colony then had a series of military deputy governors till Colonel Thomas Davey's administration (1813–17), followed by that of William Sorell (1817–24). None of these men set a good example in terms of moral conduct and it was common for military and civilian officers to take convict women as mistresses.

Children received little or no education in this primitive penal colony at the edge of the world, though an Orphan School was established by the government. Such few respectable families as there were usually employed an educated convict to teach their children. As time went on private schools were established to educate those children whose parents cared about or could afford schooling.

Van Diemen's Land, it must be stressed, was perceived as a penal colony first, last and always. During Sorell's administration more convicts continued to arrive. They numbered about 5500 males and 550 females, a proportion of men to women which was to remain about the same during the entire era of transportation to 1853.

> AUCTION of a WIFE!—A Hibernian whose finances were rather low, brought his wife to the hammer this morning, and although no way prepossessing in appearance, to the amazment of all present, she was sold and delivered to a settler for one gallon of rum and 20 ewes. From the variety of bidders, had there been any more in the market, the sale would have been very brisk!

Nothing could better illustrate the moral tone of early Van Diemen's Land than this extract from the Hobart Town Gazette *of 1 March 1817.*

Punishments could be harsh if convicts misbehaved, but generally speaking the prisoners were treated well if they behaved themselves, largely because the government and settlers depended so completely on their labour.

As the new colony expanded it was faced with a continual shortage of workers. The convicts, in their role as assigned labourers to the colonists, were therefore in a relatively strong bargaining position. The fate of the assigned labourer depended on how he or she was treated and on individual weaknesses and strengths on the part of both master and convict.

Consumption of alcoholic liquor was enormous in this isolated and male-dominated colony. As in New South Wales, alcohol was part of a primitive system of barter. Central to the primitive economy was the commissariat store. This was conducted by the government and bought provisions such as wheat and flour, lamb and beef from private settlers in order to give out food rations to the ever-increasing number of prisoners and government officers.

By selling at an agreed price to the commissariat, numerous enterprising settlers, convict and non-convict in origin, made a great deal of money. For these people the colony of Van Diemen's Land led to a substantial step up in the world. They came to associate their fortunes with the island and had pride in being from Van Diemen's Land.

Questions for discussion

1 It is said that some 4000 years ago the Aborigines of Van Diemen's Land ceased eating scaled fish. Why do you think this was? How might we go about finding the reason?

2 If possible, examine Aboriginal artefacts in the Hobart or Launceston museum or, failing that, illustrations of them. What do they reveal about the nature of Aboriginal culture? How do you account for the absence of the boomerang and spear-thrower and, for that matter, the bow and arrow?

3 Why did the British occupy the island of Van Diemen's Land in 1803–4 and not earlier or later?

CHAPTER 2

The Colony Fully Established

Black War

AS ENGLISH COLONISTS continued to occupy the pastoral areas of Van Diemen's Land, they encountered increasing resistance from the Aborigines. Frustrated and then bewildered by the realization that the Europeans were there to stay, the black people fought back for the land over which they had moved for so long.

Their lack of numbers prevented mass attack on the enemy but there is evidence that the Aborigines resisted strongly and adopted tactics to defend themselves. They singled out individual whites or small groups for attack. Sometimes an isolated house or hut was surrounded and the whites driven out by setting the roof on fire. In their dwellings some Europeans made loop-holes through which to shoot at the besiegers.

An Aboriginal woman named Walyer, from the north-west part of the colony, became a feared adversary. She taught the Aborigines how to use firearms and kill Europeans, and said she liked the invaders about as much as a black snake.

With the trial and public hanging of three Aborigines in 1825 and 1826 for the murder of Europeans, it became apparent that the English meant business.

In contrast to the treatment of the Aborigines, no European was ever brought into court to answer charges for killing Aborigines. This was largely because no white would give evidence against a fellow white and because martial law made the murder of Aborigines 'legal'. In addition the invaders, with few exceptions, considered the Aborigines as less than human and as pests, hindering their ability to occupy fully the land.

Following the declaration of martial law, search-and-destroy missions were organized by private settlers and units of the army. This new tactic was entirely ruthless: any Aborigine in the settled districts was at risk of being shot on sight.

Van Diemen's Land was an extremely violent society, with or without the presence of enemy Aborigines. The Europeans were also utterly determined to exploit the resources of the colony to the full. Everything that stood in the way would have to go, whether it was Aborigines, native flora and fauna, or anything else perceived as an obstacle to colonization.

In 1829–30 Governor Arthur organized a line of soldiers and civilians to 'beat' the Aborigines like hunted animals into the confined area of the south-west, on Forestier Peninsula. This campaign was a demonstration to the free settlers of official government power. Although only two Aborigines were captured, it brought home to the black people the fearsome power of the invaders.

Arthur accompanied this by appointing G. A. Robinson, a settler, to try to calm the remaining Aborigines. This Robinson did in a series of dangerous and wearying journeys through the colony. It was ironic that he was helped by several Aborigines who, perhaps naively, perhaps realistically, threw in their lot with Robinson and trusted him.

George Augustus Robinson was employed by Governor Arthur between 1829 and 1834 to gather in the Aborigines who remained in the bush. Those giving themselves up were sent to the Furneaux Islands.

He came to understand, up to a point, the various Aboriginal languages and by the early 1830s had rounded up the depleted black people. He persuaded and forced them to take shelter from the rage of the settlers by going on to the Furneaux Islands. The Aboriginal people, or what remained of them, were established in a form of concentration camp at Wybalenna on Flinders Island.

At this stage it may still have been possible for the few remaining Aborigines to recover. However, little effort was made to understand and encourage them. Disease and forced 'civilizing' proved a lethal combination. Numbers decreased and few remained when the government at last brought them back to their native land and settled them on D'Entrecasteaux Channel. Here indifference once again was the order of the day and the survivors of a once-coherent culture were forced into lethargy, drunkenness and vice.

Some of the descendants of the Aborigines continued to live on the Furneaux Islands in primitive conditions, engaging in the mutton-bird industry. Other people of Aboriginal origin, greater in number than once was thought or admitted, had settled elsewhere

Neglected and demoralized Aborigines were brought from Flinders Island to Oyster Cove on D'Estrecasteaux Channel in 1847.

in the colony, keeping a low profile. Only in recent years has a sense of identity emerged. Both white and black now express more interest in the Aboriginal people and a culture which was largely the victim of European colonization and aggression.

Governor Arthur

George Arthur was Governor of Van Diemen's Land, 1824–36.

Governor George Arthur presided over Van Diemen's Land for no fewer than twelve years from 1824, much longer than other governors of the colony. He was an ex-soldier and gained experience in administration elsewhere in the Empire before arriving at Hobart Town accompanied by his wife and family. He was, and remained, the soul of respectability and efficiency.

In 1825 the government of Van Diemen's Land was formally separated from that of New South Wales and Arthur reigned supreme, answerable only to his masters at the Colonial Office in London.

A man of frugal habits and sober state of mind, Arthur stood in marked contrast to his predecessors and their irregular style of life and government. The new governor took it as his sacred duty to organize his penal colony so that vice would be punished and virtue rewarded.

Given the free and easy men he had followed, this made Arthur extremely unpopular among the unscrupulous land owners and merchants, who considered that the colony was there for them to exploit to the utmost. Arthur, on the other hand, was always mindful of his duty to use the convicts to the best advantage of the British government, and to discipline them so that transportation would become a feared punishment at home.

Arthur's power was made even greater by his final say in who should or should not be offered free land grants. Until this system was abolished by the British government in 1831, the settlers were forced to please Arthur if they wanted land or convict labourers.

The governor cracked down hard on incompetent public servants too. Many of them had been placed in positions of trust and responsibility which they systematically and skilfully abused in order to line their own pockets. Arthur got rid of them or transferred them whenever he could.

London gave the governor a free hand providing that the convict system appeared to be working successfully and providing that he did not break down under the enormous strain of administering Van Diemen's Land. Arthur was a workaholic and an evangelical, supporting religion whenever he could. His was a civilizing mission and he was greatly aided by the fact that Van Diemen's Land was enjoying an economic boom. In addition, the population was growing in leaps and bounds as a result of immigration of convicts and free settlers, as well as natural increase.

During these early years there was continual tension between the demands of conducting an efficient system of convict labour and meeting the needs of the growing number of free settlers, who resented living under the tight military and civil control that Arthur found it necessary to enforce.

The governor objected strongly to moves for some form of colonial house of parliament and fought against the establishment of a non-censored press. He saw this move as something that would encourage convicts and trouble-makers to resist the measures he considered necessary for the effective running of the penal colony.

During Arthur's period of government, the wool industry began to flourish. With the encouragement of British textile interests, the number of fine-wooled sheep increased greatly. Van Diemen's Land wool-growers imported high-quality sheep directly from such places as Saxony and so raised the quality of their flocks and hence their amount of wealth. The midlands emerged as an excellent area for the production of wool.

With the removal of the Aborigines, the path was cleared for thorough exploitation of that area. Settlers came to achieve a sense of permanent settlement and developed strong economic interests in their properties and in the colony.

There was little manufacturing industry. In many ways Van Diemen's Land appeared to be the ideal colony: a place to be used as a source of primary (agricultural and natural) products to be exported home, a source for the sale of British manufactured goods, and a spot where Britons might immigrate and prosper through the availability of a plentiful and cheap labour force of convicts.

Hobart Town grew swiftly as an entrepôt port—a place for temporary storage of goods in transit, administrative centre and principal home of importing businesses. By the end of Arthur's regime, the all-important currency had been brought under the control of the government and business became more efficient as English sterling money replaced the earlier chaos of coins in circulation—Johannas, ducats, gold mohurs, pagodas, Spanish dollars, rupees and guilders.

The north flourished too, the original settlement at the mouth of the Tamar having been moved to Launceston, nearer the rich agricultural and pastoral areas.

By the mid-1830s it appeared that all the pastoral areas of Van Diemen's Land had been occupied. The mountainous and inhospitable west attracted no one. The heavily-forested north-west, north-east and Huon were not suitable for wool-growing.

Certainly the far north-west was settled in 1825 by the Van Diemen's Land Company, based in London, but in the mistaken belief that fine wool could be produced there. Wool production was not profitable in such an area of high rainfall. Small-scale timber production began but the easy pickings which every colonist sought were not there.

In these circumstances, enterprising colonists from Launceston cast their eyes across Bass Strait, and in the 1830s began occupying the area known as Port Phillip and Australia Felix. John Pascoe Fawkner, who as a child had been with Collins's expedition to Port Phillip in 1803, was one who perceived opportunities across the water. John Batman, also son of a convict, anticipated rewards, too.

Thus the restless Van Diemen's Land settlers came to the new land, full of bounce and self-importance. Known as the 'Gumsuckers', they expressed great contempt for New South Wales 'Cornstalks', who came south into the area, also intent on exploitation.

The Convicts

It is unknown how many Van Diemen's Land settlers, free, freed or escapees, made the short and usually rough voyage to the new settlement in Port Phillip. Evidence in the form of the convict origins of many present-day Victorians, and shipping lists, suggests that it was substantial, even before the gold rushes.

The convict system was at the centre of Arthur's Van Diemen's Land. Having reorganized and systematized the voluminous records the system created, Arthur was satisfied that he had complete dossiers (documents) on each and every person transported. By use of these records he was able, through his Convict Department, to oversee the entire deployment of the vast labour-force. Although government officers and magistrates looked after the various districts into which Arthur divided the colony, the governor always had the final say.

Transportation of convicts had different and sometimes conflicting aims. In essence, it was designed to punish, to reform and to deter. Deterrence was based on the assumption that evil-doers would be put off committing crimes at home for fear of a sentence of transportation handed down by British courts.

There is no way of knowing whether the theory worked or not and, short of asking citizens of Britain why they had failed to become criminals and be transported, there could be no answer. It is impossible to know whether law-breakers feared a sentence of transportation. There is flimsy evidence in the form of ballads warning prisoners about the fate of transportees but convicts did not know for sure whether they would be transported if sentenced,

THE
TRANSPORT'S

Letter to his Father and Mother at Bolton, in Lancashire.

Hobart's Town, Van Diemen's Land,
December 14th, 1829.

D*ar Parents,*

I embrace this opportunity of writing, hoping these lines will find you well. With respect to myself I have little to say, and shall not here disguise the truth. I have been most miserable in this unhappy land; I have suffered every deprivation of life, insult upon insult have been heaped upon me; I have been obliged to associate with the most depraved of human beings, my Master's men. Separated from all hope of comfort or enjoyment, debarred from all religious worship, I have been ready to murmur at the decrees of the Almighty. What can I say to you? I am living one hundred and fifty miles from Sidney, up the mountains, forty miles from any place of worship The voice of prayer is never heard, and all is blasphemy and wickedness; and I have to lament in the field at all kinds of toil, under a meridian sun, and am become alike indifferent to comforts of all kinds. When I am hungry I eat, when I am thirsty I drink—I receive my mess as another. We grind in a hand-mill, we bake in the ashes, and live in miserable huts, which admit both wind and rain. A sheet of cork and a bundle of straw is our bed, and a blanket is our covering; but fatigue is ours, and we sleep as well as on beds of down. A shirt and duck trowsers form our dress. I have learned to reap, to shear sheep, to fell timber, to burn it off—in short I can do almost all laborious work. Gracious God! could the rising youth but have a single glance of the prisoner in New South Wales, they would surely shun the temptation to crime. The slightest offence provokes flogging; insolence is the bugbear of the colony; for this I have been sent to an ironed gang, to work in chains,

COPY OF VERSES.

Come all you wild and wicked youths, wherever you may be,
I pray you give attention and listen unto me.
The fate of us poor transports, as you shall understand,
The hardships that we undergo upon Van Dinman's land,

Young men all now beware, Lest you are drawn into a snare.

My parents rear'd me tenderly, good learning gave to me,
Till by bad company was beguil'd, which prov'd my destiny,
I was brought up in Lancashire, near Bolton town did dwell
My name it is young Henry, in Chorley known full well.

Me and five more went out one night, into a 'Squire's park,
Hoping we could get some game, the night it proved dark,
But to our great misfortune they trepanned us with speed,
And sent us Lancaster, which made our hearts to bleed.

It was at the March Assizes to the bar we did repair,
Like Job we stood with patience, to here our sentence there,
There be up some old offenders which made our case go hard
My sentence was for 14 years, was quickly sent on board.

The ship that bore us from the land the Speedwell was her name,
For full five months, and upwards, boys we plough'd the foaming main.
Neither land nor harbour could we see, believe it is no lie,
All around us one black water, boys above us one blue sky.

and to be half famished, or tied up to receive the ignominious punishment of sixty or seventy-five lashes. Shame on the name of Englishmen! A man who calls himself a settler, first imposes upon his slaves, and goads them on to speak, and then drags them before a magistrate to be lashed and tortured for insolence. If a slave speak, the wretch's stomach is taxed. We all feel a tenfold degradation here; we feel that we are slaves to paltry tyrants, who seem as if they were born to add to the stings and tortures of wretched criminals. If a Government servant sees his master's property going to ruin, it is ten to one but he passes on, and takes no notice—he argues that it is no business of his, and thus the settler, by not studying his men's interest, forgets his own. The men receive no wages, and not sufficient clothing. The Authorities will say— "Why do you not complain to us, we will remedy it." But do you think that any will, or dare complain, when the Authorities will support the Settler, and that the Master is sure to take his revenge! Tea, sugar, and tobacco, are called indulgences, and rest with the discretion of the Master, who never forgets to use his power like a giant. With respect to liberty, it is a thing that few now get possession of. A lifer must serve eight years with one Master, ten with two, and one year added for every additional master. The smile of bitterness comes over my face whilst I write this: may God enable me to overcome this sensation. Why is man debarred all chance of liberty, whose conduct may be irreproachable? Much of the misery and crime committed by convicts may be attributed to the almost total extinction of their hope of liberty, As to myself, I once did think of a mitigation, but all hopes are gone; I am like a piece of mechanism; my spirit is so much broken by disappointments and hardships,

that I feel a dreadful indifference creep upon me—my life appears a blank, and futurity is my only source of expectation. One step alone appears before me; I shall consider of it twelve months, and then take my election.

Immediately upon my landing in September, 1830, my fellow-sufferers and I were assigned to settlers up the country. The master I was then assigned to is still living, and I can have his testimonials as to the blamelessness of my conduct. I have also the strongest testimonials of good conduct during our passage. The Superintendent was very anxious to gain me some situation suitable to me, but the letters he wrote to the Secretary were neglected by the chief mate, who was to send them on shore; and as I was in consequence assigned to my present employer, as his Excellency had signed it, and it could not be reversed.

My health is much impaired, but complaints are in vain. I am sorry to inform you that poor Chas. Fallows was lately executed at Sydney in company with five others, for being concerned in the robbery and murder of their master and mistress. But although such executions are frequent, the repetition of crime is daily occurring. We are not permitted to see a newspaper, and indeed, if we are seen to converse much with each other, it is ten to one but we are either dragged before a magistrate and punished with a severe flogging, or else some of our provisions are stopped. I hope and trust you will make this letter as public as possible, and that it may be the means of turning them from their present dishonest practices, is the earnest prayer of your unfortunate Son,

Henry James.

When you write to me direct in the same manner as you sent the last.

I often look'd behind me, towards my native shore,
That cottage of contentment, there I ne'er shall see no more,
Nor yet my own father, who tore his hoary hair,
Likewise my tender mother the womb that did me bare.

The fifteenth of September, then we did make the land,
At four o'clock we went on shore, all chained hand to hand,
To see our fellow-sufferers, we felt—I can't tell how,
Some chain'd unto a harrow, and others to a plough.

No shoes nor stockings they had on, nor hat they had to wear
But a harden frock and linsey drawers, their feet and head
were bare,
They chain'd them up by two and two, like horses in a team,
Their driver he stood over them with his Malacca cane.

Then I was marched to Sidney town, without any more delay,
Where a gentleman he bought me his book-keeper for to be,
I took this occupation—my master liked me well,
My joys were out of measure then I'm sure no tongue can tell.

We had a female servant, Rose-anna was her name,
For fourteen years a convict was, from Liverpool she came,
We often told our tales of love, when we were blest at home,
But now we're rattling our chains, in a foreign land do moan.

H. Wardman, Printer, Bradford.

and certainly did not know whether New South Wales or Van Diemen's Land would be their new home.

The convict's destination was largely a matter of chance, except in Ireland. All convicts from there were, till 1840, sent to New South Wales only and the reason for this remains a mystery. One result was that Van Diemen's Land was established as a strongly Protestant colony.

Arthur tried hard to make transportation a dreaded punishment, but he was only partly successful. The problem was that a convict in Van Diemen's Land could, if he or she behaved reasonably well, be released quite early and be permitted to work for wages or start a business. Some became very rich indeed and it is possible that stories of success that got back to England far outweighed in the public mind the cases of failure. Van Diemen's Land undoubtedly presented many opportunities for a fresh start if the convict were at all resourceful. A decent master was an additional bonus.

An important point is the youth of the prisoners. Most received a seven-year sentence and many did not serve it all out. This meant that men and women were frequently in their late 20s when released. The world lay before them.

Nearly all transported convicts were eventually freed. Unfortunately documentary records provide little information after this point. It is only in recent years that their descendants have expressed an interest and genealogists uncovered material long unknown, concealed or guessed at.

It must be understood that, in the eyes of the people of the time, the convict was not transported for trivial offences. The shock treatment of removing criminals from environment and associates was probably the aspect of transportation that did most to reform criminals.

The typical convict to Van Diemen's Land was male, from an urban area, in his early 20s, with little skill in a trade, and transported for some form of theft. Poachers, long said to have been the typical convict, were few and far between.

Such was the saturation of Van Diemen's Land by convicts that, by the late 1830s, at least four out of every ten people in Van Diemen's Land were currently convicts in the total population of about 45 000. There were about 77 000 people in New South Wales. The overall population of all the Australian colonies was perhaps 125 000, with small numbers in the infant colonies of Western Australia and South Australia.

Many more were of convict origin and knew it. The fact did not trouble them much. There was a careless pride in their new land among the inhabitants of the island colony who, in their own judgement had done well. This sense of local sentiment, however, was always tempered by a sense of being British.

Associated with the healthy economic situation and rapidly increasing population was a dark side. The basic penal character of the colony was never out of sight or mind, in somewhat the same way as the plantation-owners of the southern states of the United States were always aware of the slave basis of their culture, economy and way of life.

There existed in Van Diemen's Land two worlds, that of the free and freed and that of the prisoner. There was always, in a penal colony, the element of brutalization. It was ever-present in the forms of discipline and punishment which inevitably were part and parcel of a system of convict-dominated life and labour.

Punishments were handed out freely. For misconduct, the prisoner was formally tried by the magistrates or at a higher court of law, depending on the seriousness of the charge. Courts handed down sentences of jail, work in an ironed gang, fines or flogging for offences such as petty theft, being absent from work, insolence, idleness or disobedience.

Established in 1830, the Port Arthur penal settlement was closed in 1877, when its surviving inmates were transferred to Hobart Town. Visible here is the semaphore pole: signals were sent to other stations on Tasman's Peninsula and as far as Hobart Town by moving the semaphore arms into various positions.

Women convicts presented a special problem in punishment. Though in the early years of settlement, women were flogged, the usual punishments for misconduct were a spell in the female factory, hard labour at the wash tubs or, in some cases, shaving of the head. Serious offences committed by men, such as inflicting grievous bodily harm or systematic and serious theft or robbery, housebreaking or burglary, were punished by sentences to Macquarie Harbour penal settlement or from 1830 on, to Port Arthur.

At these places of secondary punishment, the discipline was extremely severe. Particularly during the early years, public executions were quite common. Dramatic highlights of life, and death, within the convict system figure in Marcus Clarke's melodramatic novel *For the Term of His Natural Life* and in stories by Price Warung. Clarke's depiction of convict life as it was generally experienced is quite misleading but it remains a grim reminder of what could occur.

On the positive side, good behaviour by the prisoner was normally rewarded with a ticket of leave after a few years of assignment. This permitted the freed convict to work independently for wages or at a trade, on condition that regular reports were made to the police. In this way convicts either worked out their full sentence or became free by award of a pardon.

Pardons were usually conditional, the condition being that the convict did not return to Britain. An absolute pardon restored the convict to full rights of a British citizen, and was awarded to mark some especially praiseworthy conduct, such as deeply impressing the master and government with excellent and lengthy good behaviour or, perhaps, saving a life or risking death in a rescue attempt.

The crucial point about the transportation system is that it supplied a continuous and steady labour force for the colonization of Van Diemen's Land. Public buildings, roads and bridges were continually under construction by convict work gangs. Private houses were built with convict labour. Settlers were dependent on convicts in a thousand and one ways, from female cooks and governesses, to stone-masons, carpenters and unskilled labourers, to clerks and shepherds.

The wealth and prosperity of the island colony were built on the foundations of a highly organized system of forced labour.

Government

In the short but turbulent period to 1853, Van Diemen's Land continued to be a penal colony, but side by side with convict transportation there was also immigration of working class Britons and those who had a little money.

Tension between the demands of a penal colony and the expectations of the free, be they humble or powerful, led the governors into many difficulties. Arthur resisted demands for a free non-censored press, but was finally and reluctantly forced to grant it when New South Wales did. He also resisted trial by jury.

Female immigration to Van Diemen's Land in the 1830s was entrusted largely to the London Emigration Committee. The chief agent John Marshall was also a shipowner and contractor, and he had an arrangement with this Committee for chosen emigrants to travel in his ships; he was paid £16 a passenger.

(opposite)

At first this important mark of a free society was limited to military juries, on the grounds that there were too many unqualified and prejudiced people from whom to draw a jury of the respectable. Gradually pressure from local colonists and increasing liberal feeling in Britain obliged Van Diemen's Land governors to permit full trial by jury if it was asked for. Being selected for service on a jury came to mark the acceptance of men as respectable colonists. No women sat on juries.

During the period to the 1850s, the power of the governor of the colony was gradually diminished. From 1825 there was a Legislative Council to assist the governor with framing local laws and regulations but it was still frequently under the thumb of the governor, especially during Arthur's time.

Legislative Council members were nominated by the governor, not elected, and included senior civil servants. Power flowed from Arthur and hence it was not surprising that his Council generally gave way to him.

In 1828 the number of members of the Council was increased as the result of a British Act of Parliament, but Arthur continued to dominate the administration of the colony, his skills and experience continually strengthening his position.

In the mid-1830s, following the passage of the great Reform Act (1832) in Britain, and amid growing opposition to such institutions as slavery, doubts began to be raised about continuing transportation side by side with the increase of free settlers in New South Wales and Van Diemen's Land, and the proposed free settlement of South Australia.

In 1837 a committee of the House of Commons, chaired by Sir William Molesworth, paraded before the public and parliament horrifying instances of ill-treatment of convicts in Australia. This evidence was carefully chosen to discredit transportation and any benefits it may have had.

The Colonial Office had virtually decided to end transportation even before the Molesworth committee produced its lurid findings and so it was that in 1840 the assignment system came to an end in both Australian penal colonies.

Yet transportation as such was not abolished to Van Diemen's Land, though the organization was altered. The new arrangements were dubbed the probation system. Under it convicts were no longer to be assigned to private settlers but lodged in labour camps, under discipline. In theory, as their conduct progressively improved, prisoners were to be made available to the settlers at hiring depots.

This plan misfired because an economic depression drastically reduced the demand for labour (on which the success of the probation system depended), too many convicts were poured into Van Diemen's Land, and free settlers became upset at the bad name that the island continued to bear, as a penal colony.

Female Emigration

TO

AUSTRALIA.

10

COMMITTEE:

EDWARD FORSTER, Esq. *Chairman.*	CHARLES HOLTE BRACEBRIDGE, Esq.	CHARLES LUSHINGTON, Esq.
SAMUEL HOARE, Esq.	JOHN S. REYNOLDS, Esq.	GEORGE LONG, Esq.
JOHN TAYLOR, Esq.	JOHN PIRIE, Esq.	COLONEL PHIPPS,
THOMAS LEWIN, Esq.	CAPEL CURE, Esq.	NADIR BAXTER, Esq.
	WILLIAM CRAWFORD, Esq.	S. H. SHERRY, Esq.

The Committee for promoting the Emigration

OF

Single Women

To AUSTRALIA, under whose Management the Ships "Bussorah Merchant and Layton" were last Year despatched with Female Emigrants, acting under the Sanction of His Majesty's Secretary of State for the Colonies, HEREBY GIVE NOTICE, That

A Fine SHIP of about 500 Tons Burthen,

Carrying an experienced Surgeon, and a respectable Person as Superintendent to secure the Comfort and Protection of the Emigrants during the Voyage, will sail from

GRAVESEND

On Thursday 1st of May next,

(Beyond which day she will on no account be detained) direct for

HOBART TOWN,

VAN DIEMEN'S LAND.

Single Women and Widows of good Character, from 15 to 30 Years of Age, desirous of bettering their Condition by Emigrating to that healthy and highly prosperous Colony, where the number of Females compared with the entire Population is greatly deficient, and where consequently from the great demand for Servants, and other Female Employments, the Wages are comparatively high, may obtain a Passage

On payment of FIVE POUNDS only.

Those who are unable to raise that Sum here, will be allowed to give Notes of Hand, payable in the Colony within a reasonable time after their arrival, when they have acquired the means to do so, as they will have the advantage of the **Government Grant** in aid of their Passage.

The Females who proceed by this Conveyance will be taken care of on their first Landing at Hobart Town; they will find there a List of the various Situations to be obtained, and of the Wages offered, and will be perfectly free to make their own Election; they will not be bound to any person, or subjected to any restraint, but will be, to all intents and purposes, perfectly free to act and decide for themselves.

Females in the Country who may desire to avail themselves of the important advantages thus offered them, should apply by Letter to "The Emigration Committee, London," under Cover addressed to "The UNDER SECRETARY OF STATE, COLONIAL DEPARTMENT, LONDON." It will be necessary that the Application be accompanied by a Certificate of Character from the Resident Minister of the Parish, or from some other respectable persons to whom the Applicant may be known; but the Certificate of the Resident Minister is in all cases most desirable. Such Females as may find it expedient may, when approved by the Committee as fit persons to go by this Conveyance, be boarded temporarily in London, prior to Embarkation, on Payment of 7s. per Week.

☞ All Applications made under cover in the foregoing manner, or personally, will receive early Answers, and all necessary Information, by applying to

JOHN MARSHALL, Agent to the Committee, 26, Birchin Lane, Cornhill.

EDWARD FORSTER, *Chairman.*

NOTE. The Committee have the satisfaction to state that of 217 Females who went out by the Bussorah Merchant, 180 obtained good Situations within three Days of their Landing, and the remainder were all well placed within a few Days, under the advice of a Ladies' Committee, formed in the Colony expressly to aid the Females on their arrival.

LONDON, 22nd February, 1834.

By Authority:
PRINTED BY JOSEPH HARTNELL, FLEET STREET, FOR HIS MAJESTY'S STATIONERY OFFICE.

The long-standing tension between the needs of the free settlers and the needs of the penal system grew. Governors of Van Diemen's Land came under highly emotional attack but the British government persisted in its policy of sending criminals to the island.

In 1842 New South Wales was granted a reformed Legislative Council which included some elected men representing the wealthy. This reform was not granted to Van Diemen's Land because it continued as a penal colony. Such denial of an elected government and representative institutions further angered the free colonists in the island at the same time as they associated their economic misfortunes with the transportation system.

Governor Arthur was transferred from Van Diemen's Land in 1836. On his way down to the Hobart Town wharf to board ship for home, this administrative genius and most successful governor astonished onlookers when he suddenly burst into tears at leaving the island he had controlled with a hand of iron for twelve years.

Questions for discussion

1 What were the causes, course and results of the 'Black War'?

2 To what extent was Aboriginal culture damaged or destroyed by the 1830s?

3 Why were convicts transported to Van Diemen's Land? What happened to them?

4 In what ways did Van Diemen's Land fulfil its role as British colony?

CHAPTER 3

Tensions and Depression

New Governors

Sir John Franklin was governor of Van Diemen's Land 1837–43, and encouraged education, the arts and science in the colony.

ARTHUR'S REPLACEMENT was Sir John Franklin, the hero of polar exploration and said to be a favourite of King William IV. If this was so, when the King died in 1837, Franklin lost his most powerful patron.

The new governor was accompanied by his energetic wife, Lady Jane Franklin, and together they set out to advance the culture and education of the people. Franklin went out of his way to encourage interest in state and church schools and was very active in establishing Christ's College, for the sons of ladies and gentlemen.

Surrounding themselves with men of learning and underwriting the Tasmanian Natural History Society, Sir John and Lady Franklin worked to bring the benefits of modern thought and science to the colony. Lady Franklin especially, stood in marked contrast to Governor Arthur's wife, who had been fully occupied with family duties and conscious of her secondary role as a female, even if the wife of a governor.

Lady Franklin made herself conspicuous by undertaking journeys of exploration to the forbidding west coast, by establishing a museum (Acanthe) at what became known as Lenah Valley on the outskirts of Hobart Town and by encouraging free settlement in the Huon area. More than that, she far exceeded the customary woman's role by involving herself in the government to such an extent that she was finally suspected by the Colonial Office of actually drafting official reports to London.

Franklin was a generous man but he irritated senior public servants by his lack of expertise and a rather vague way of being well-meaning. He became isolated in his job and floundered, coming heartily to wish he had never heard of Van Diemen's Land.

Finally the Colonial Office gave the governor no choice but to resign and this he did in 1843.

Franklin's successor was Sir John Eardley Eardley-Wilmot, an English gentleman deeply interested in crime. He had a rich field for research in Van Diemen's Land, but the economic depression of the early 1840s, the problems related to the new probation system, and his style of life brought him criticism from his superiors in London.

The free settlers sensed that the days of transportation and cheap labour were numbered and became more and more uneasy at the influence of transported convicts on their society and homes.

Conflict arose between Eardley-Wilmot and the new head of the Church of England in the colony, Bishop Nixon. They quarrelled on the issue of who should appoint clergymen to minister to the spiritual needs of the convicts. Eardley-Wilmot won on this point but at the cost of becoming the enemy of Nixon and senior Church of England people.

The governor gave further ammunition to his critics by the careless and undignified way in which he was said to conduct himself with women. His wife had remained in England and the expert character assassins of Van Diemen's Land had a field day circulating rumours about the governor's alleged over-familiarity with certain colonial women.

In London, the new and ambitious secretary of state for the colonies, W. E. Gladstone, aided and abetted by his powerful under-secretary, James Stephen, determined that Eardley-Wilmot must go.

These two were fed information by church dignitaries from Van Diemen's Land. Gladstone grew alarmed that the governor of that far-off island was not providing enough information about the reform of prisoners and their moral state, matters which Mr Gladstone took keenly into account. There was also concern about the level of education being given to the rising generation of Van Diemen's Land.

Altogether, Eardley-Wilmot was not making a good impression. He was dismissed in a despatch from London beginning with the fatal words, 'It is my painful duty to inform you . . .'

Gladstone went on his way to higher things. The governor died in Hobart Town a few days after the arrival of his successor, Sir William Denison.

Denison was an engineer by profession and very well-connected socially in England. A skilful and highly intelligent man, he settled a conflict in his Legislative Council only to be faced with a determined onslaught by the opponents of transportation.

Opposition to Transportation

Taking very lofty moral ground, colonists such as the Reverend John West of Launceston and the Launceston *Examiner* became the centre for this opposition to the continuation of the convict system. They bombarded the London press and the Colonial Office with dark stories about the state of morality in Van Diemen's Land where, according to them, Satan was reigning unimpeded. The Anti-Transportation League was formed. Equipped with a flag featuring the Southern Cross, it set out to gain support from the other colonies and formed a powerful pressure group.

The Reverend John West (1809–73), an English Congregationalist minister, came to Van Diemen's Land in 1838. He helped to found the Launceston Examiner in 1842. He was leader of the anti-transportation movement, and his elegant History of Tasmania *reflects West's opposition to transportation; it is also a notable work of literature and learning. In 1854 West became editor of the* Sydney Morning Herald.

In the flag of the Australasian League for the prevention of transportation (usually called the Anti-Transportation League), 'Tasmania' was used to avoid the association of 'Van Diemen's Land' with convicts.

(right)

Denison continued to explain and confirm the wisdom of transportation, but with the discovery of gold in Victoria spectacular monetary inflation set in, and London became aware of the huge costs of running the transportation system. There was a certain amount of dithering by the British government which further annoyed the colonists, but in 1852 the last convict ship for Van Diemen's Land left England, arriving at Hobart Town on 26 May 1853.

News of the end of transportation after fifty years was cause for great celebration among the colonists. Denison, however, predicted economic disaster when the British funds which accompanied transportation suddenly ceased. He was proved right and the difficulties of the colony were increased by an exodus of people from Van Diemen's Land to Victoria, and emigration of British settlers to Melbourne instead of the island colony. The colonists considered an era had ended, marking the occasion by official dinners and the like and also with an official change of name from Van Diemen's Land to Tasmania. With such a ritual gesture a new start was to be made.

Two significant events occurred in 1853: the end of transportation of convicts and the fiftieth anniversary of the European settlement of Van Diemen's Land. At the Jubilee Festival, Hobart Town, people served themselves to food from the two long tables (left), and then sat down to eat (right).

In 1851 London made arrangements for a greatly enlarged Legislative Council in Van Diemen's Land and this body set about devising a constitution for a new Tasmania which would be a self-governing colony within the Empire.

Simultaneously, New South Wales, South Australia and Victoria were engaged in the task of constitution-making. All colonies worked out bills to be sent to London for consideration by the English parliament. In 1855 Tasmania learnt that its constitution had been approved.

The form of government decided upon, and still in existence today, was a two-house (bicameral) parliament, a governor, a judiciary and a civil service.

The right to vote in the House of Assembly was to be given to adult males who occupied property valued at £10 a year. In 1900 the vote was extended to all adult males and, early in the twentieth century, to female adults as well.

The Legislative Council stayed an elite body. Candidates were obliged to show evidence of wealth, and voting for the Council was restricted to certain property owners and men with above average education. Electorates were roughly similar in the number of people they contained but soon became extremely unbalanced. The Legislative Council had substantial power indeed and no arrangements were made for it ever to be dissolved.

Religion

During this period of transportation, all the main churches came to be supported by state aid based on a formula related to their number of worshippers. The Church of England, although favoured in some respects, never had the degree of authority and influence it did in Britain.

The nature of the penal colony militated against the strengthening of religious feeling because from first settlement clergy were associated with the convict system. They sat as magistrates, handed down punishments and generally were seen as part of the system which forced convicts to attend church.

In addition, clergy were not always of upstanding character or inspired by the Christian message. The first Anglican minister, the Reverend Robert Knopwood, achieved a reputation for hunting, shooting and fishing in the eighteenth-century style.

The Reverend William Bedford replaced the Reverend Knopwood as minister of St David's, Hobart Town, in 1823. Bedford laboured hard in his difficult position in the penal colony but lost it to the Reverend Phillip Palmer in 1833. Bedford also thereby lost his seat in the Legislative Council, which did not please him. A smouldering quarrel between he and Palmer did nothing to raise the church in the estimation of the people, already aware of Bedford's habit of running up bills and, in 1836, falsifying records of his visits to schools.

When Bishop Nixon came in 1842, Bedford resented his right to preach at St David's. Nixon retaliated by padlocking the door against Bedford, who then resourcefully secured the services of a man who could deal with locks.

The Catholic Church was served in Van Diemen's Land by the Reverend Phillip Conolly, who arrived in 1821. The Catholic inhabitants of Van Diemen's Land had been eighteen years without an officially appointed priest.

Father Conolly was inclined to be eccentric but did his best under the circumstances. He built St Virgil's chapel on a site later to be occupied by St Mary's Cathedral, but fell out with his superiors when Bishop Polding found fault with his conduct, Conolly actually suing his bishop for defamation.

With the arrival of Bishop Robert Willson in 1844, the Catholic church was much strengthened at the same time, as the convicts began to include large numbers of prisoners from Ireland. Willson went in for charitable work and he and Nixon did a good deal to raise the prestige of their respective churches.

The Reverend Archibald Macarthur came to Hobart Town in 1822, the first Presbyterian minister in the Australian colonies, but in 1835 he admitted guilt to charges seriously affecting his moral character and returned to Britain.

Early Methodist clergy came to Van Diemen's Land in a spirit of eager missionary enterprise and were encouraged by Arthur. They were seen by the governor as excellent men who did not fear to go among the convicts; William Horton made a particular point of preaching at the hospital and gaol in Hobart Town.

A Turning-point

By the mid-1850s Van Diemen's Land/Tasmania had arrived at a turning-point. Transportation of convicts had ended, a form of self-government was being ushered in, and the people looked forward to a bright future.

They had become used to continual prosperity through the investment and spending of British money on the convict system, wool and wheat growing, and whaling. The depression of the early 1840s was seen as merely an unfortunate event, never to be repeated. The boom of the gold-rush period led to huge exports of such items as timber at greatly inflated prices which masked economic change.

Some fifty years had passed since the first European occupation of the island. The Reverend West wrote a splendid two-volume *History of Tasmania* and had it published in Launceston.

To all intents and purposes, it seemed that the colonization of the island had triumphantly succeeded. Hobart Town was the second city of all Australia, though rivalled by Launceston with its important trading link with Melbourne.

Encouraged by the demand for building materials in Victoria, and bark for tanning at Launceston, colonists began to occupy the river-mouth areas of the north-west. Freed convicts moved into the new area.

In the Huon as elsewhere in Tasmania, subsistence farmers began their struggle with the bush, preoccupied with getting what their parents and grandparents had never had—the prized possession of land. For the free and the freed, land was an obsession. Ownership of it was thought to be essential if the settler, or at least his children, were to go up in the world and do well. In modern terms, to have land was a great status symbol.

Parliament, reflecting government ideology, encouraged people to go on the land, thereby further reinforcing the value placed on it. Every acre was to be made fruitful if it were at all possible because the immigrant-settlers had emerged from a Britain or Ireland where people generally did not own land and never would. In the colonies it was going to be different.

In 1855 the population of the new free colony of Tasmania was about 70 000 out of a total Australian population of about 600 000. New South Wales and Victoria had about 220 000 people each and South Australia 80 000. In comparison with her earlier population position, before the gold discoveries, Tasmania was rapidly falling behind.

Economically too, the island colony was giving way as the gold boom on the mainland drew the attention of new capital as well as new immigrants. No precious metals were discovered in the island, secondary industry lagged and the colonial governments entered a period when they were hard-pressed to balance their budgets.

A lengthy period of economic depression cast its shadow over the formerly prosperous colony. Population increased slowly in comparison with other colonies (with the exception of Western Australia) from the 70 000 in 1855 to 114 000 in 1880. Imports and exports dropped to record lows in the late 1860s, as did the all-important government revenues from custom duties, a main source for government funds at a time when no income tax was collected.

A sense of despair and a lack of confidence stood in remarkable contrast to the energy and spirit of adventure which had been typical of the early years.

Opinion of Visitors

Visitors noticed the prevailing mood, and found little to praise except the temperate climate. In the mid-1860s the prominent English political figure Sir Charles Dilke visited Tasmania in the course of a world tour. He recorded seeing half the houses shut up and deserted, and acre after acre of old wheat land abandoned to the scrub.

This was blamed on the Tasmanians' poor system of agriculture. There was no attention paid to crop rotation, it was reported by Dilke, and little effort to introduce steam and other improved agricultural machinery. A disease called fluke ravaged the sheep flocks, he continued gloomily, and there was a ruinous hand-to-mouth system of agriculture.

Dilke spoke of the dead hand of the convict past. Others blamed Tasmania's woes on the withdrawal of British capital associated with the convict system and the failure to discover gold, on the lack of interest in public affairs displayed by the gentry or on the effect of absentee landowners.

Visitors were the more impressed with the lack of energy in the colony because it contrasted so sharply with the beauty of the island's landscape and the number of superb mansions erected by the wool kings and the wealthy town dwellers. Many noticed the similarities of parts of Tasmania to parts of England and then pointedly contrasted the energy and prosperity of Britain with the lethargy of the island colony.

In 1861 the Reverend Dr Frederick Jobson, a visiting clergyman, reported that Launceston was a town of some 10 000 inhabitants. Its streets and shops were in the more level part, extending down to the wharf at the edge of the water. The sloping elevations around the town were sprinkled over with the dwellings of what Dr Jobson described as the genteeler class, and were tastefully adorned with gardens and vineyards.

In the middle of the town was a fine open square with ecclesiastical structures at the sides, and a Paris bronze fountain in the middle. Launceston was a pleasant and picturesque town, concluded the visitor, and truly English in character.

This 1858 view of Brisbane Street, Launceston's main street, shows the Georgian architectural style of the buildings. The watercolour artist, Frederick Strange, was a convict who arrived in Van Diemen's Land in 1838; he was granted a conditional pardon in 1849.

(detail)

The next day at 5 a.m. Jobson left for Hobart Town in a four-horse coach, which ran daily in fourteen hours from Launceston to the capital. The road was very good, he enthused, having been made by convict labour and having had no amount of necessary work spared from it.

Dr Jobson was reminded of the coaches which bowled along the Great North Road in England. En route, towns and villages with their cottages, houses, shops, gardens and churches all looked as if they were English. He remarked also on the prevalence of gardens colourful with English primroses, pansies, cowslips, daisies, violets and geraniums. In many gardens were English beehives too.

This was very much the English colony then, but there were also signs of more local characteristics when some kangaroo hunters got on the coach and began yarning about their kangaroo dogs and the size of the 'boomer' kangaroos to be found in the interior. Dr Jobson was impressed by stories of 'boomers' four or five feet high, able to bound a dozen yards at a time and, when brought to bay, fighting desperately with their backs against a tree, so that they could not be seized from behind.

Dr Jobson's fellow-passengers also told him of possum shooting by moonlight and the peculiar habits of the wombat or 'badger', as it was known in the colony. The hunters proclaimed themselves well acquainted with the haunts of the Tasmanian eagle which, they said, destroyed new lambs. They had seen the emu running wild; they spoke of shooting swans, pelicans, cormorants and penguins, as well as hawks and vultures.

Hobart Town, the visitor found, contained about 20 000 inhabitants. It had good well-paved streets lined with large shops and stores, and was adorned with fine public buildings. The heart of the city, went on Dr Jobson, was on the lower ground near the river. Cottages, villas, terraces and gardens covered the sides and crests of seven hills which bounded the capital of Tasmania.

The large harbour was exceedingly safe and commodious and had many good warehouses at its head. Like all tourists, the visitors were struck by the domination of Mount Wellington, a picture of sombre magnificence. At the water's edge were markets, newspapers, cab-stands and so on, much on the pattern of English towns of a similar size. In all, rejoiced Dr Jobson, Hobart Town offered unmistakable proof that it belonged to Great Britain.

Typically he was told tales of the convict period and was impressed that, even so, it was common for people in lonely parts to leave their doors unlocked at night.

It was a feature of the post-transportation period to insist that Tasmania was now suddenly 'respectable'. The knowledge and shame of what had been done led the people to distance themselves from the past. It was probably this effort which led to pride in being seen to be more English than the English.

Loyalty to Britain

Loyalty to Britain, then, was not surprising. After all, Tasmania was a British colony, peopled by settlers who were British in origin. Its institutions and even appearance were British, as Jobson and many another visitor saw.

Sport followed British patterns, even to hunt meets. Horse racing was enjoyed as in England and so were cricket and aquatic sports. The currency in circulation was British, with the likeness of Queen Victoria on it. People were reminded of their colonial status and British connection every time they posted a letter because again there was a portrait of the Queen on the stamps. The post offices in Hobart Town and Launceston were most substantial and important buildings, at least in part because they were a crucial link with home.

Holding his riding crop and top hat, this 'man of the turf' exemplifies how English sport was enthusiastically adopted in Van Diemen's Land. The artist C. H. T. Costantini, a troublesome but talented prisoner, was a convict transported in 1827.

The governor of the colony was English and the clergy usually came from Britain. The dominant social position of the Church of England and its form of worship were constant reminders of England. The loyal toast preceded the business of official dinners and occasions, and the Queen's birthday was officially marked in Tasmania.

The very remoteness of Tasmania rendered the loyalty of the colonists even greater. The Crimean War led to astounding manifestations of loyalty, and huge sums were donated to a fund for the wives, children and widows of British soldiers killed or wounded in that campaign. For many years Tasmanians took great pride in remembering how much they had given.

The visit of Alfred, Duke of Edinburgh, in 1868 was seen as a highlight in the history of the colony, Tuesday, 7 January, being the day of that ever-to-be-remembered-year upon which the first scion of English royalty set foot on Tasmanian soil.

Enormous numbers of people turned out in Hobart Town. Triumphal arches were constructed, public and private buildings decorated. At night there were brilliant illuminations and a torch-light aquatic procession on the Derwent.

His Royal Highness went by coach to Launceston where he was met by the principal citizens at the site of a grand triumphal arch on the Wellington Road. From there the procession went along Wellington to Frederick Street, to St John Street at the junction of which, beside St John's Church, about 3000 Sunday School children, with their teachers, were assembled on an immense platform specially constructed for the purpose.

The streets were strewn with bouquets of beautiful flowers. At night the Town Hall and public buildings were splendidly illuminated. The fronts of the houses in most of the streets were decorated with brilliantly and tastefully executed designs produced by using transparencies and gas lighting, which had been installed in the northern centre eight years earlier.

Such was the welcome to a son of Queen Victoria—and when an attempted assassination in Sydney failed in its object because a bullet was deflected by the royal braces, Tasmanian colonists were as outraged by the attack as any loyal Britishers could be.

Even as the native fauna were being slaughtered, as reported to Dr Jobson by the kangaroo hunters he met on the coach, it was being replaced with species from home. Sir Charles Dilke was one of many who reported with a mixture of amusement and amazement the huge efforts being made to acclimatize English salmon. This feat was finally accomplished and Tasmanians congratulated themselves on thus importing a fine fish.

Deer were also introduced. So were many plants that later turned out to be weeds in the colonial context. The blackberry was one such example and those who brought it came to be heartily cursed by later generations.

Joseph Archer's property 'Panshanger', four kilometres east of Cressy, is one of the finest colonial houses in Tasmania. It was built in the early 1830s.

An even more damaging import was the rabbit. No one was able to control it till the mid-twentieth century and the damage it did is incalculable. Already by 1870 it had reached pest and plague proportions. The spread of this most destructive of mammals in Tasmania was probably aided by the clearing of rain forests.

Introduced animals endangered some of the fifteen native species of birds in Tasmania, which were forced to compete with such foreigners as starlings and sparrows. The sugar glider (flying possum) was brought to Launceston from Port Phillip in the 1830s and foxes let loose at Stanley in 1854.

Of the local fauna, the emu was wiped out by about 1873. The Tasmanian tiger (thylacine) was said to destroy sheep and a bounty of 10s. a scalp was placed on it in 1840 by the Van Diemen's Land Company. Between 1888 and 1909 more than 2000 thylacines were slain for the bounty alone. There have been no confirmed sightings of the animal for more than fifty years.

Much more tragic was the decline of the Tasmanian Aborigines. In 1869 William Lanney, said to be the last full-blood male of his people, died. At this time learned societies in England were interested in obtaining specimens of the skulls of Aboriginal people.

Trugernanna, born about 1812, came from Bruny Island. She lived until 1876, and was the last full-blood female Aborigine in Tasmania.

Lanney's death was accompanied by ghoulish scenes when the body was mutilated allegedly for scientific purposes. When Trugernanna died in 1876 her body too came to share a similar shameful indignity when the skeleton was kept as a curiosity. Much too late the European colonizers came to show interest in the people they had removed from the scene.

The education of young Tasmanians was closely based on the English curriculum. Attendance at school was made compulsory in 1869 but enforcement was lacking. For many years parents removed their children according to the demands of harvest time or other similar reasons for using children for cheap labour.

Fees were paid to the teachers, but in hard times this source of income diminished, even for parents who placed value on the education of children beyond learning the rudiments. Not all did, and the demands of colonial life and the constant heavy physical work it involved left education a poor second in the list of priorities.

Teachers were frequently not very well educated themselves and the only training as a rule was through the monitorial system. Young people learnt on the job, as it were, or simply 'picked up' teaching little children as if it were a simple trade. This was a system in which one bad teacher could set bad examples for years and years to the monitors. Innovation and advancement in education was made extremely difficult.

Government Policy

In the thirty years or so after the granting of self-government, Tasmanian ministries rose and fell on local issues. The economic depression prevented much government spending as the colony marked time.

Tasmanian governments tried to add to the income from customs duties by borrowing funds on the London money market. This and the sale of primary produce, especially Tasmanian wool, further locked Tasmania and the other colonies, into British interests. As substantial debts were built up in London an increasing proportion of government income had to be earmarked for repayment of interest to British money-lenders. These arrangements were par for the course in colonial Australia and adopted generally as financial policy.

Tasmania's secondary industry did not develop because of its small population of consumers and free trade policy. This made the island colony especially vulnerable to taxes on its exports levied by colonies such as Victoria.

Strenuous efforts were made by Tasmanian governments to create an inter-colonial free trade zone between the colonies, in the belief that Tasmania had nothing to lose and a great deal to gain.

Government expenditure was trimmed to a point where the day-to-day running of government was in danger. Moves to impose a form of income tax were defeated. The Legislative Council made itself conspicuous by vetoing any progressive legislation which emerged from the House of Assembly and waiting for something to turn up.

One ray of sunshine was the discovery in 1871 of deposits of tin ore at Mount Bischoff. James 'Philosopher' Smith found these, and export of tin looked set to become an important primary industry. Gold was also found but production of the precious metal never looked like reaching the enormous output of the Victorian diggings.

Another way forward to prosperity was glimpsed in the construction of railways. Due to the energy of northern colonists, the railway age did at last arrive in Tasmania. The Launceston–Deloraine line was commenced in 1868 when the Duke of Edinburgh graciously turned the first sod on 15 January. This line was financed and managed by local people under government guarantees. The enterprise was greeted with resentment and jealousy in the south.

Unfortunately for the promoters, the line did not pay and when the government stepped in and attempted to recover its money in 1874 there were riots in Launceston. At this, the government drew back.

About the same time, a railway line from Hobart Town to the north was proposed, to be built by the government this time. The decision further irritated the north but the coming of the railways did lead to increased employment for a while, if not the anticipated miracle for agriculture and business.

Yet things did pick up a little in the 1870s. More stable government and less feuding was one factor. Another was increased British investment in the Australian colonies, a trend which was to reach its height in the next decade.

Health

Though every visitor exclaimed that the climate of Tasmania was excellent, especially in the summer when tourists from the mainland made their way to the coolness of the island colony, disease and illness became a serious factor in the everyday life of the settlers and their families.

In parts of Hobart Town and Launceston housing was atrocious and over-crowding the order of the day. The lack of water sewerage systems became more serious as the urban population increased. Outbreaks of typhoid began to worry doctors.

Although it was realized that low-lying areas were more dangerous to health than elevated sites, germ theory was as yet unknown. People thought that disease was connected to what they termed a miasma. Doctors were limited in their power to cure or control illness, although chloroform came to be used to limit the pain suffered by patients undergoing surgery.

People did well to keep out of hospitals. Vaccination was encouraged by progressive physicians and those who interested themselves in health as a public measure, but there was resistance. People feared that the vaccination itself was dangerous. Contagious and infectious diseases were treated by isolating the victims but frequently this step was resisted. Often the damage was done by the time isolation was accepted.

Many mothers had their babies delivered by midwives whose skill and knowledge had been learnt the hard way or from folk medicine. Infant mortality was extremely high in relation to later figures, and it was common for a new baby to be given the name of an earlier sister or brother who had died in infancy.

Questions for discussion

1 What were the main factors which led to the abolition of transportation of convicts?

2 In what ways did the colonists of Van Diemen's Land/ Tasmania reveal their British heritage?

3 How would you go about assessing the effects of convict transportation on Van Diemen's Land/Tasmania?

4 Try to look over some National Trust properties. Why were they selected for preservation? What do they tell us about life in the colony?

CHAPTER 4

Prosperity

I N COMMON with her fellow colonies, Tasmania enjoyed a period of considerable prosperity and optimism in the 1880s and indeed into the 1890s, despite the depression of that decade.

Land Settlement

Extension of land settlement was a feature of the latter part of the century. Development of agriculture rather than pastoralism was the key-note. Prospective farmers were encouraged to tackle the heavily-forested land of the north-west, north-east and Huon areas.

Land legislation basically reflected the idea that the 'natural' wealth and prosperity of Tasmania came from its soil and that the virgin land was there to be exploited.

During this period especially the forests of Tasmania became home to numerous sawmills. Timber resources were thought to be virtually unlimited and Tasmanian axemen became extremely expert in their occupation. An entire sub-culture developed around the Tasmanian bushmen-axemen. Their skills and daring were exhibited at many a carnival.

The problem for governments and people so enthused with this idea of close settlement was the actual cost of creating an idyll of smiling meadows, ripening crops and a happy and contented yeomanry. Nevertheless, so important was land settlement considered to be that provision was made for low repayments on the cost of the land. Numerous efforts were made to ensure that the new settlers stayed on their blocks of land and did not sell them unimproved.

The huge forests of the north-west, those of the north-east centred on Scottsdale, and other such areas revealed the fertility of the ground from which the forest giants grew to such amazing dimensions. During the last thirty years of the nineteenth century enormous effort went into clearing the land.

This (undated) scene illustrates the density of much of the Tasmanian bush and the difficulties settlers had in trying to establish themselves. Note the 'corduroy' road necessary in the wet climate, and the tree stumps which indicate the massive trees.

Blocks of crown land of fifty acres and upwards were offered for sale, but the lack of roads made life extremely difficult for the settler. Timber markets in Victoria encouraged some clearing in mid-century but the favoured method was ring-barking trees to stop their growth and then either burning them or grubbing them out.

These methods called for the exercise of great muscle power on the part of both the settler and his family, and their bullocks. Professional bullock drivers developed great skill in shifting fallen logs and trees and piling them into heaps or rows. When sufficiently dry they were set on fire in the autumn.

Painfully the forests began to be cleared. The first settlers in these areas sought to keep alive by running a few cows and a pig or two and growing such crops as could be planted out among the forest tree-stumps. Potatoes were found to thrive in the soil of the north-west and dairying also began to be developed in areas of suitable rainfall, especially in the north of the colony. Seed grass was sown and gradually paddocks emerged. At first the divisions between them were frequently huge piles of logs formed to make fences, then post-and-rail fences and eventually barbed wire.

Primitive houses were built from timber split on the spot. Roofs were made from shingles and very large fireplaces bricked in. The wife of the family sought to grow vegetables in a home garden and the children were regarded as an integral and important part of the farm economy because they did not require payment. Some children were obliged to trudge very long distances to school, if there was one, or to get there on horseback.

There was little prospect of a drought occurring. Water was gathered from the rain off the roof or perhaps sledged from a creek in barrels.

Meals were all heavily based on consumption of lamb, beef, pork, or chicken. If there were a few cows, butter could be made in the primitive dairies. Large quantities of tea washed down the meat-three-times-a-day diet.

Lighting was by candle or kerosene lamp. Transport was by horseback or some conveyance such as a trap along treacherous and dangerous roads through the bush. Carting potatoes out and down to the coastal wharves was usually done by horse- or bullock-drawn wagons and was especially difficult and slow in wet weather.

In many areas places of worship were built, with the Methodists particularly strong along the developing north-west. Churches were a social centre. More frequently hotels were established and formed an important part of the social scene, particularly for men. Bargains were struck, gossip exchanged and news of the day passed on. Women might be catered for in one room of a hotel, but generally it was not considered proper for a woman to go into a hotel.

Work

The settler on the land in late nineteenth century Tasmania might succeed in scraping a living, hoping for good prices for his produce, or he might not. A good deal depended on whether he could tide himself over by running up credit. Essentially success or failure or simply hanging on was closely related to market prices of produce.

Heavy and hard physical work was necessary, but for those who secured good fertile land and had a series of good seasons it was possible to make money with surprising speed.

For most of the century, in the urban areas of the colony, few women worked outside the home, apart from those who were employed as shop assistants, school teachers and, as time went on, post mistresses. There was, however, some important seasonal work available at the jam factories established by Henry Jones and Company in the south. Hop-picking became a time for families to work together in the hop fields, even children being taken in prams. Fruit-picking was another seasonal job.

Girls and young women were expected, and themselves expected, to marry in their early 20s or earlier, and henceforward form part of a family group in which the husband and father was the breadwinner.

Although work was hard and hours long for virtually all Tasmanians, the biggest and most constant share was borne by

Hops were grown mainly in the Derwent Valley from the 1820s, and around New Norfolk from 1834. Generations of families lived and worked on the hop fields, and in the harvest period even quite young children participated.

housewives. With few or no labour-saving devices, they reared children, did the washing, prepared meals, sewed and generally slaved in what was seen as their God-given role.

Many men were employed in the traditional trades of carpentry and building and various work associated with metals. Employment as a clerk or shop assistant was regarded by some as an upward step and banking was considered particularly prestigious. Road trusts (set up before local government was established) also provided work, as did the need for domestic servants for wealthy householders.

For many people the only time they had off was Sunday, and not always that. In urban slums such as Wapping in Hobart, people were largely untouched by civilizing influences.

At the lower end of Collins Street, Hobart, near the waterfront, was the slum area of Wapping. Through it ran the Hobart Town Rivulet, which for much of the nineteenth century was little more than an open sewer.

Collection: TASMANIAN MUSEUM AND ART GALLERY

(detail)

In this colonial economy there was always unemployment in the towns or, at best, seasonal work only. Statistics were not coherently kept, if at all, but those seeking employees could always tap a pool of the unemployed.

Perhaps an arrangement would be made in a pub or perhaps those out of employment would go from place to place, moving from one employer to another. In these circumstances, a reference or 'character' assumed enormous importance. In small settlements, the reliable and the unreliable would be known by word of mouth, but in other cases a stranger would not be taken on until extensive enquiries were made.

No unemployment benefits existed. The down-and-out could at best hope to be supported by relatives, or at worst by private charity. Many overlapping networks developed. A churchgoer might put in a word to a friend after the service for a man known to be seeking work; a shopkeeper doing well might let it be known to others who were 'letting a man go' on account of bad business that he was on the lookout for a good employee.

During this period not only the north-west and north-east areas were settled. In the Huon district apple-growing was found to be profitable when the problem of cooling fruit for export overseas was solved. Despite the scourge of the codlin moth, production increased rapidly. It was the appearance of Tasmanian apples on the British market that led to the colony becoming known as 'the apple isle' in England.

Minerals

The west coast of the colony was little known in 1880. The convict settlement at Macquarie Harbour in the 1820s led to the gathering of some timber by the men held captive there, but such was the extremely rugged nature of the country, inhospitable climate and heavy rainfall that it was quite unsuitable for pastoral or agricultural expansion.

A general picture of the area became available from 1862 when the government geologist Charles Gould entered the Linda Valley and named Mounts Owen, Jukes, Sedgwick, Huxley, Darwin and Lyell after the British scientists concerned in the dispute about evolution caused by the publication in 1859 of Charles Darwin's *Origin of Species*.

The discovery of tin at Mount Bischoff in 1871, finds of alluvial tin in the north-east in 1874, and the firing of the Launceston tin smelters the following year, led people to conclude that more mineral wealth might lie hidden in the colony.

Prospectors struggled south and west in search of a lucky strike, returning to the settlements on the coast in winter or when their supplies ran out. In 1879 tin and gold were found at Mount Heemskirk.

Meanwhile James Crotty, a prospector, in 1883 came on a deposit called the Iron Blow which turned out to overlay a fantastically rich deposit of copper. A jetty at Trial Harbour was constructed. In 1892 the Mount Lyell Company was established, and by the end of the 1890s a smelting process was being employed and numerous private companies had been formed.

In 1885 the government geologist learnt that silver had been identified at a wild spot near Mount Zeehan. Reports of gold discoveries filtered through. Silver-bearing ore was located at Mount Dundas and by 1890 a township of more than 2000 people had sprung up and been named Zeehan.

Railways were laid into this difficult region to tap the huge copper resources. The port of Strahan developed and Captain Napier Bell, an engineer, ingeniously improved the entrance to Macquarie Harbour. Here at Hell's Gates, as it had been known to the convicts, a training wall of rocks and other works deepened the water and enabled the entry and exit of ships of more than tiny size.

The Abt railway was laid near Mount Lyell in 1896. This type of railway, named after the German inventor, was built in mountainous country and used a third or middle rack rail with cogs on it. The train engine drove a pinion wheel which gripped the cogs and so pulled the train.

As the mining companies flourished and the town of Queenstown boomed, fumes from the smelting process and the necessity to secure firewood created a strange landscape at Mount Lyell.

Various plans were made to communicate with the area by rail from the Derwent valley or from the vicinity of Deloraine. The area was too rough, however, for the laying down of railways except at prohibitive cost, although the Emu Bay Railway Company did run a line through to Burnie.

By the beginning of the twentieth century the production of blister copper, tin, gold from Beaconsfield, Mathinnna and Lefroy, and silver had helped change the economic profile of Tasmania almost beyond recognition.

Accompanying the mining boom was a substantial increase in population from 101 000 to 183 000 from 1870 to 1899. Value of exports in the same period quadrupled to £2.6m. In 1899 the total population of the west coast was 25 000.

New Political and Social Ideas

On the political scene there was also a feeling of optimism. Modern liberal ideas from Britain and Victoria came to the island colony, brought largely by new immigrants. Governments of the day began to move away from the earlier policies of doing the minimum possible in terms of government services.

Government-appointed boards of health co-operated with local government and doctors to control or prevent outbreaks of infectious diseases. Sewerage works and proper street cleaning and drainage began. Information came from other parts of the world on how preventive medicine and measures for better hygiene in the preparation and distribution of food could improve the health of the people.

With the lighting of part of Launceston by water-driven power turbines, Tasmania ushered in the age of electricity.

An Education Act of 1885 followed the other colonies and British and American educational theory in trying to make provision for effective free, compulsory and secular education, but its powers were not fully used. Attendance remained a problem, partly because local education boards were a stumbling block. Members of these local bodies were reluctant to prosecute parents they knew.

The new arrangements nevertheless formed a bridge from the old go-as-you-please system. What was to be termed the 'new education' was introduced early in the twentieth century.

A university was founded in 1890 and the first lectures delivered three years later.

First housed in 1863, the Tasmanian Museum and Art Gallery was extended in 1880 and 1901. In Launceston, the Queen Victoria Museum and Art Gallery was expanded in 1891 and shortly afterwards vested in the Launceston Corporation.

During this period of reform and optimism, trade unionism developed slowly in comparison with the other colonies, in part due to lack of large secondary industries with the number of workers necessary for effective action. Enthusiastic Labour men visiting the colony were shocked at the poor working conditions and the want of progressive thought among the workers.

With the huge mining developments, however, came new concepts. Workers began to respond to leaders who urged that the toiler should be represented in parliament by one of his own number; however, the Labour movement as a whole remained submerged in liberalism. The notion that trade unions should negotiate wage claims on behalf of the workers was disapproved of as an infringement of people's liberty and right to make what bargains they could. The eventual organization of trade unions reflected the death of the idea that all men were equal in the market place to bargain about wages and conditions of employment. Concurrently there was a growing realization that some ground rules should be enforced in areas such as prevention of disease, work conditions and education.

In 1893 the radical *Clipper*, published in Hobart, dedicated its cheeky columns to political consciousness-raising among the workers. Modelled up to a point on the Sydney *Bulletin*, it made its voice heard, and tried to demolish Tasmania's reputation as a sleepy hollow where the workers were bluffed into being paid less than in other colonies for the same work.

Towards the end of the decade and on into the new century, the distress suffered by the labouring classes during the 1890s depression led some to turn in due course to a Labor party. This movement was influenced by the sharper cutting edge of similar movements on the mainland.

Tasmanians, however, sensed not a class war but a conflict of Tasmanians versus mainland interests of all sorts, and particularly in the field of shipping on which they depended for all imports and exports.

The collapse of the Bank of Van Diemen's Land in 1891 was a blow particularly felt by mining interests, which were being lent money by it. Worse was to follow as bank collapses elsewhere, and especially in Melbourne, led to a sense of anxiety followed by severe unemployment.

Private charities and the government tried to find employment for those thrown out of work. Tasmania, along with the other colonies, recovered from these problems towards the end of the 1890s.

A certain amount of optimism survived, however. The mining industry remained generally viable in those hard times and there was spirit enough to promote the tourist trade. Perhaps to encourage a picture of beautiful Tasmania, the government became the only one in Australia to issue scenic postage stamps.

War

Tasmanians continued to be strongly imperialistic during this period. The colony's weak position in the event of an attack reinforced local feelings of patriotism, which reached new heights during the Empire-wide celebrations to mark the 1887 and 1897 jubilees of Queen Victoria's accession to the throne in 1837.

News of the death of General Gordon at Khartoum in 1884 sent a thrill of loyalty through the community, and in 1899 the outbreak of the Boer War led Tasmania to offer contingents to serve in South Africa. Leading Tasmanian colonists were convinced that if Britain was at war then Tasmania must loyally join in. About 1000 Tasmanian volunteers went to the Boer War out of a total Australian force of about 16 000, at a time when the colony's population was 173 000 out of Australia's 3.8 million.

Troops are farewelled before departing for the Boer War.

Federation

A feeling of insecurity was one reason for the desire to form a federation with the other states. Great notice was taken of a senior British army officer who strongly recommended that the colonies bring together their six colonial military forces into one defensive unit.

There were other reasons as well for federation, but in Tasmania's case especially there was the strong opinion that a form of union with the other colonies could only help the island's economy.

There were referendums on federation. In 1898 the Tasmanian vote for 'yes' was 12 259 and 2820 for 'no'. In 1899 the figures were 13 437 and 791 respectively. About 47 per cent of electors did not vote one way or the other in the two votes.

TAKE THIS HOME WITH YOU.

THURSDAY,

27th JULY, 1899

IS A

HOLIDAY

WHY ?

In order that as many as possible of the Electors may record their VOTES for the great cause of

AUSTRALIAN FEDERATION.

THIS DAY

Will be a famous day in years to come ; for on this day Tasmania will become part of

A Great and Free Nation !

TAKE THIS HOME WITH YOU.

John Vail, Government Printer, Tasmania.

Tasmanians such as Andrew Inglis Clark played a part out of all proportion to Tasmania's size in the campaign that led to federation. Essentially the island colony wanted its defences locked into those of the other colonies and its trade with them freed from tariff impositions.

Clark was very active in drafting the wording that was eventually to lead to a constitution, but neither he nor any other Tasmanian wanted a fully unified nation. They held that the island's interests would be swamped by the larger states.

As it turned out, other colonies felt the same way when confronted with the power and population of New South Wales and Victoria. Nearly a hundred years of European settlement strengthened Tasmania's sense of itself as an island entity, chilly in the shadow of the mainland's size and apparent indifference.

Further, where the other colonies traded with each other by land and sea, Tasmania's sea-link only made its colonists doubly keen for a guarantee in relation to free trade.

Tasmanians were convinced that they would do well out of federation. The result was a most powerful federal sentiment in the island, checked only by the feeling of some that the financial arrangements of the new federation might not be all they should be. Some of these fears were removed when it was agreed to return a fixed proportion of money from the federal government to the state governments. Two votes on federation were held in the colonies in 1898 and 1899. In both, Tasmanians voted by a huge majority to go into the federation.

Questions for discussion

1 What difficulties were encountered by the new settlers on the land?

2 What were the principal minerals discovered in Tasmania? How were they mined and where were they sold? What problems did the mining industry encounter?

3 Why did Tasmanians vote as they did in favour of federation? Who opposed it, and why?

CHAPTER 5

Advances and Reversals

I N THE FIRST TWENTY YEARS of the twentieth century, Tasmanian history was marked by further reforms and the foundation was laid for industrialization. Then a catastrophe overwhelmed the state when the Great War broke out.

Education

In this classroom at Calder Road school (1906), there are no individual desks. Presumably the bicycle in the corner belonged to the teacher.

In 1904 the government secured the services of W. L. Neale, an educationalist from South Australia. The report he wrote on the deficiencies of the state education system led to his appointment as Director of Education the following year.

Neale had a good deal to do. The Depression of the 1890s had led to extensive school absenteeism because impoverished parents found it impossible to pay fees. The government was loath to abolish these charges since the money would then have to be raised through higher taxes.

School papers had been introduced among the senior classes but the curriculum was unimaginative. Slates were still in use. 'Drill' was the only form of physical education and the movements of children at it presented a sad sight. 'Singing' was little more than a hideous medley of notes, though the pupils evidently enjoyed it.

Neale set about advancing the new education. This removed the emphasis from rote learning and authoritarian teaching. It sought instead to encourage the development of every side of a child's nature. Young Tasmanians were, under Neale's guidance, to be prepared for life in all its aspects.

Unfortunately for Neale, his plans for wide-ranging reform and teacher training led him into conflict with the more conservative teachers and, though he tried to conceal the fact, Neale did not suffer fools or opponents gladly. He had a brusque style and offended people by his impatience.

The new director upset Tasmanians by bringing in teachers from South Australia and allegedly appointing some of them over the heads of locals. It is little wonder that Tasmanian teachers reacted with a good deal of jealousy. Of some 500 employed, no fewer than 350 had no formal training at all. Their ability to motivate children in the new education was minimal, Neale concluded.

The atmosphere was turbulent and some politically powerful Tasmanians were very irritated at being told that their education system was less than perfect. Neale probably overstated his case but he did succeed in founding an all-important training college for teachers. He also persuaded parliament to make attendance at school free, and gained approval for the building of a kindergarten, though work did not start on it till 1911.

Ragged schools, such as this now-derelict one in lower Collins Street, Hobart (about 1920), were organized in Hobart and Launceston for the children of the very poor, in an effort to keep them off the streets.

Collection: TASMANIAN MUSEUM AND ART GALLERY

Opposition to Neale redoubled. Hostility to his reforms was based in the Legislative Council where members correctly concluded that their work—or lack of it—on local boards of advice was under attack.

Parliamentary opposition proved too much. Following royal commissions into his running of the Education Department, Neale resigned and returned to South Australia.

He was succeeded by W. T. McCoy, who built on the foundations laid by Neale. Previously an inspector in New South Wales, McCoy had also imbibed the new education, but turned out to be a much more skilful diplomat than Neale.

McCoy succeeded in establishing larger and more ambitious primary schools. State high schools were opened in Hobart and Launceston in 1913, followed by two intermediate high schools at Devonport and Burnie a few years later. In this work McCoy was fortunate in that from 1914 to 1916 he had a progressive Labor Minister for Education in the person of J. A. Lyons, himself an ex-teacher.

Reform

New labour movements in the state were organized through Workers' Political Leagues and similarly named organizations. Their development was greatly aided by the formation of Labor Parties in New South Wales and Victoria and the presence of Labor candidates in federal elections.

In 1906 seven Labor men were elected to a House of Assembly numbering thirty-five members. In 1896 Andrew Inglis Clark introduced a proportional representation system of election at the local government and House of Assembly levels in Hobart and Launceston. This meant that each party was awarded a number of seats in proportion to the number of votes for its candidates. Country seats remained single-member constituencies.

The next year an Act provided for the election of all members to the House by proportional representation, the state being divided into five constituencies, each with six members. In 1909 the first election using the federal divisions was held on this basis. It became known as the Hare-Clark system. The Legislative Council kept single-member constituencies.

The power base of the new labour movement tended to be among west-coast miners. Many came from the mainland and brought with them a sense of working class cohesion and political liveliness which was largely unknown before. In 1911 there was a major strike on the Lyell field.

Coupons such as this were issued by the A.M.E.A. during the 1911 strike at Mount Lyell, and were accepted as payment by shops and hotels and cashed at the union office. The strike lasted 56 days.

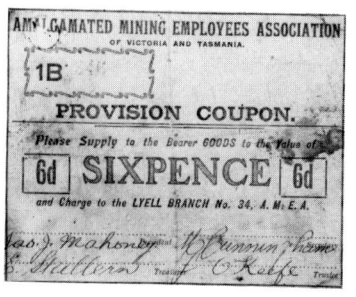

The Mount Lyell smelters were started in June 1896, and officially opened the next year. Horse-drawn wagons brought in thousands of tons of machinery from the coast during a period of eighteen months.

By bringing together workers and employers, Wages Boards (created in 1911 and reorganized in 1920) regularized pay and conditions in factories and shops for trades or groups of trades having a common link. This step also sharpened the political consciousness of workers.

The object of this legislation was to improve the conditions of factory workers, including women, young persons and children. It was also aimed at maintaining or increasing the standard of wages to a fair and reasonable level.

Generally speaking, a forty-eight-hour week was worked, with overtime rates permitted. A maximum of ten hours a day was fixed. No person under fourteen years was to be employed in any factory any more, though boys over that age and girls over sixteen could be worked fifty-five hours a week in order to meet a total workload of up to 200 hours a year. No youth under sixteen and no female whatsoever was to work after 9 p.m.

With the legislation, evidence about rates of pay emerged. In the dressmaking and millinery trade, some girls actually received nothing at all and others 2s. a week, at a time when a pair of women's shoes cost between 3s. and 5s.

Some of these workers had been badly exploited but did not try to recover lost wages for fear that they would be sacked if they dared. A milliner with eight years' experience received 12s. a week. Some employers went in for 'ringing the changes'. This was a scheme whereby women were reclassified so that their wages would not have to be increased.

Shop assistants were permitted at least a half-day holiday a week but uniform shop-closing hours proved difficult to enforce.

Attempts were made to raise the standard of factory accommodation and regularize wages to a level where employees could live decently. Even new houses, however, were small and clearly unsuitable for many families.

The health of Tasmanians also led to further reforms, especially when in mid-1903 an outbreak of smallpox terrified the inhabitants of Launceston. It also caused the cancellation of the hundredth anniversary of European settlement.

The severity of the smallpox outbreak led the government to seek help from Victoria. Dr J. S. C. Elkington came, inspiring confidence by his breezy and reassuring style in combating it. Elkington was rewarded by being made Chief Health Officer.

Dr Elkington was the scourge of both local and state governments as he documented the source of disease in still primitive or non-existent sewerage disposal, polluted water supplies, bad housing and the like. He and Neale collaborated in bringing home to teachers a knowledge of hygiene and how it was to be instilled into school children. Elkington turned out propaganda pamphlets highlighting the fact that rudimentary school and public and private buildings appeared designed only to encourage the growth of the successful germ.

Despite opposition from people who considered that any criticism was a slur on the state, its government and public servants, Elkington was successful, partly in the short term, completely in the long run.

Health officers in the Education Department awakened Tasmanians to the damage done to children, and medical study of them became a national cause. Dental health was yet to come, but when Elkington left to become Commissioner of Public Health in Queensland, he could reflect with satisfaction on the changes he had been responsible for in Tasmania.

Many advances were being made. A state Council (later Department) of Agriculture publicized modern methods of farming, particularly dairying, by use of travelling exhibitions and the production of an agricultural gazette.

Agricultural shows enabled farmers and graziers to compare and contrast their stock with that of others, but left a lot to be desired in terms of the advancement of farming as the business it was, or should have been. With the appearance of the motor car and motor lorry, as well as the motor bicycle, some rural dwellers were able to motor to such shows for the first time.

This remarkably successful film, adapted from a stage play of Marcus Clarke's novel, was made in 1908. Scenes were shot in the ruins of Port Arthur.

(opposite)

Another technical advance came in the form of moving pictures, challenging live entertainment. One of the earliest moving pictures, *His Natural Life*, based on Marcus Clarke's famous novel, reminded Tasmanians about an aspect of their past that many were still sensitive about and would have preferred to forget.

ACADEMY OF MUSIC

Direction of CHARLES MacMAHON.

A NOTABLE EVENT AND GREAT HOLIDAY ATTRACTION.

King's Birthday, Mon., Nov. 15, & Tues., Nov. 16.

POPULAR PRICES Dress Circle & Reserved Stalls, 2/6; Stalls, 2/-; Pit, 1/-.

THE PICTURE DRAMA THAT COST £1,000.

A STIRRING AND GREAT ATTRACTION !

The SUCCESS of the CENTURY.

Witnessed by 40,000 persons in Melbourne, and now

ATTRACTING ALL AUSTRALIA

New, Vivid, and Stirring Picture Drama

OF MARCUS CLARKE'S FAMOUS STORY,

On another front, local and state police were amalgamated in 1899 and a Criminal Investigation Branch established at Hobart in 1904. That year fingerprints were first taken by the jail authorities, who handed over their files and knowledge of procedures to the police in 1910.

Motor traffic began to increase. In 1905 it was made an offence not to keep to the left or nearside of an approaching vehicle or, in passing, keep to the right. Two years later the police began to handle more of the rapidly increasing work involving motor traffic. By the beginning of the Great War in 1914 there were about 3000 licensed vehicles in the state, between a half and a third of them motor bikes.

The role of the police became more and more crucial. They were obliged to deal with people who did not send their children to school, issue hunting licences, assess whether or not a closed season on certain game should be declared, inspect hotels to enforce closing time and good order, and prevent illicit gambling and betting.

After the creation of local municipalities in 1906, a range of new tasks had to be undertaken by the police. The municipalities were created to replace the confusion of bodies such as road trusts, local boards, and so on. In some rural areas the police had to take on as many as ten new activities.

Hydro-Electricity

One of the most significant developments was the establishment and acceptance of hydro-electricity in Tasmania. In the 1890s numerous schemes were proposed to use electric power on the west-coast mining fields. Then in 1910 the Hydro-Electric Power and Metallurgical Company, a subsidiary of a Melbourne-based business, became interested in producing electricity in order to process zinc ore.

They started operations the next year, with J. H. Butters appointed engineer-in-chief and manager. Under his guidance, the company built a dam at the Great Lake to generate electric power for Hobart.

Financial difficulties arose and in 1914 the Tasmanian government took over the concern under the name of the Hydro-Electric Department, headed by Butters.

On 6 May 1916 the governor-general officially opened the scheme at Waddamana. It took him three days by T-model Ford and horseback to get there from Hobart. In June the power was on. In the Hobart area, factories including the important zinc works and the carbide works at Electrona began going over to hydro-electric power. The government also acquired the electric light branch of the Hobart Gas Company's plant at the end of 1915.

Butters was a resourceful and skilled manager and the hydro-electric works went forward, the government trusting the manager and reaping the rewards of that trust.

By the end of the Great War, Butters reported that the River Ouse had been diverted into the Great Lake despite the area being isolated for some weeks by falls of snow, difficulties in transport and the problem of removing substantial amounts of rock in order to dig canals. He also noted the fact that some of his workmen were inefficient. Monetary inflation and unfavourable exchange rates with the United States (the source of certain machinery) added to his difficulties.

Butters negotiated favourable terms with the zinc company for its consumption of electric power but cautioned the government against hydro-electric development merely in the hope that business would be attracted to Tasmania. He also proposed that first of all large headworks needed to be built in the highlands during the summer months.

With this in mind, he arranged for survey parties to work out the power potential. The energetic Butters still found time to be active in the creation of the Faculty of Engineering at the University, and he looked forward to the eventual transmission of electricity to Launceston and the New Norfolk area.

By 1924, when Butters left Tasmania, by an outstanding exhibition of managerial, financial and technical skills he had set the hydro-electrification of the state on the road it was to follow.

The Great War

The outbreak of war in Europe on 4 August 1914 was greeted in Tasmania, as elsewhere in Australia, by an impressive outburst of loyalty to Britain and the Empire on the one hand, and an explosion of anti-German feeling on the other.

There was immediate unemployment in the mining industry, suddenly denied its crucial ore markets in Germany. Indeed, the war was a principal reason for the establishment of the zinc works and the desirability of securing hydro-electric power.

Of 640 men who registered in Tasmania for the army during the first few days of the war, more than half were from the west coast. State-wide, unemployment was over thirteen per cent at the beginning of 1915, compared with less than six per cent at the outset of the conflict.

Costs of food and groceries increased sharply. In response, the federal Labor government of Andrew Fisher elected in August 1914 announced a referendum to give the federal government power to control prices.

When W. M. Hughes came to office in late 1915 as Prime Minister, he at once cancelled the referendum and handed price control over to the states. The result was that the states did nothing, the Legislative Council of Tasmania having already declared its hostility to such a measure.

Hughes's action greatly irritated many Labor supporters and in the island state the Labor Premier, John Earle, further disappointed his supporters by his reluctance to grant preference in employment to trade unionists. The influence of the trade union movement on the government was limited in Tasmania and Earle soft-pedalled on Australian Labor policy.

Meanwhile people of actual or suspected German origin had their lives made a misery by Tasmania's super-patriots and those who enjoyed poking their noses into other people's business.

Anti-German propaganda was used throughout the Great War to urge Australian men to enlist in the AIF. The 'Huns' are depicted still as the barbarians of old.

People became unhinged in all the excitement of war. The town of Bismarck, originally settled by people of German origin, was renamed Collinsvale. Herbert Heaton, a lecturer at the University, was hounded out of the state because he laughed at people who wanted the entire German nation killed off. In doing this Tasmania ejected a man who subsequently achieved a world-wide reputation as an economic historian.

People lost touch with reality and believed every stupid atrocity story peddled in newspapers, which received their misleading news out of London and Paris. One of the more ridiculous stories was that Germans made soap from human bodies. The Great War rapidly became the great madness.

In March 1916 there was a state election scheduled and, at the same time, a vote on whether the hotels should close at 10 p.m. or 6 p.m., the government having already reduced closing hours from 11.30 p.m. Temperance advocates seized their chance to use war to reinforce a claim that drink was a curse and at the root of wife-beating, neglect of children, and the costs associated with jails and asylums. Early closing would lead, it was argued, to a more efficient and moral people, better fitted to work for the war effort.

The 6 o'clockers won easily. It was strongly suggested that this was due to the women's vote, but it was not simply that. Any appeal to patriotic virtue was a winner in the feverish atmosphere created by the war.

The state election caused little excitement. Labor was defeated by one seat and an Independent member, though it polled more votes than its Liberal opponents. A significant number of people who earlier voted Labor seem not to have voted at all because Labor's programme was too wishy-washy and, perhaps, because Earle had supported the unpopular 10 o'clock closing.

In somewhat the same way as the temperance people grasped the crisis of the war as an excellent opportunity to win a victory, so now did the more radical trade unionists see that the door might be opening for amalgamation and strengthening of the various trade unions in the face of official Labor compromise with the bosses.

Shattering casualties among the Australian Imperial Force (AIF) in France in 1916 gave Hughes his opportunity to push for compulsory military service. Radical Labor became ever more convinced that conscription was in reality a trick to undermine the trade union movement in the name of patriotism by bringing in female and junior workers who would be paid less than the men they would replace.

After assessing public opinion upon his return in mid-1916 from a visit to Britain, Hughes came to the conclusion that one-in all-in was the only policy for Australia if Germany was to be crushed. Like others obsessed with a single vision, he under-estimated or was ignorant of the implications for people who did not agree with his analysis of the situation.

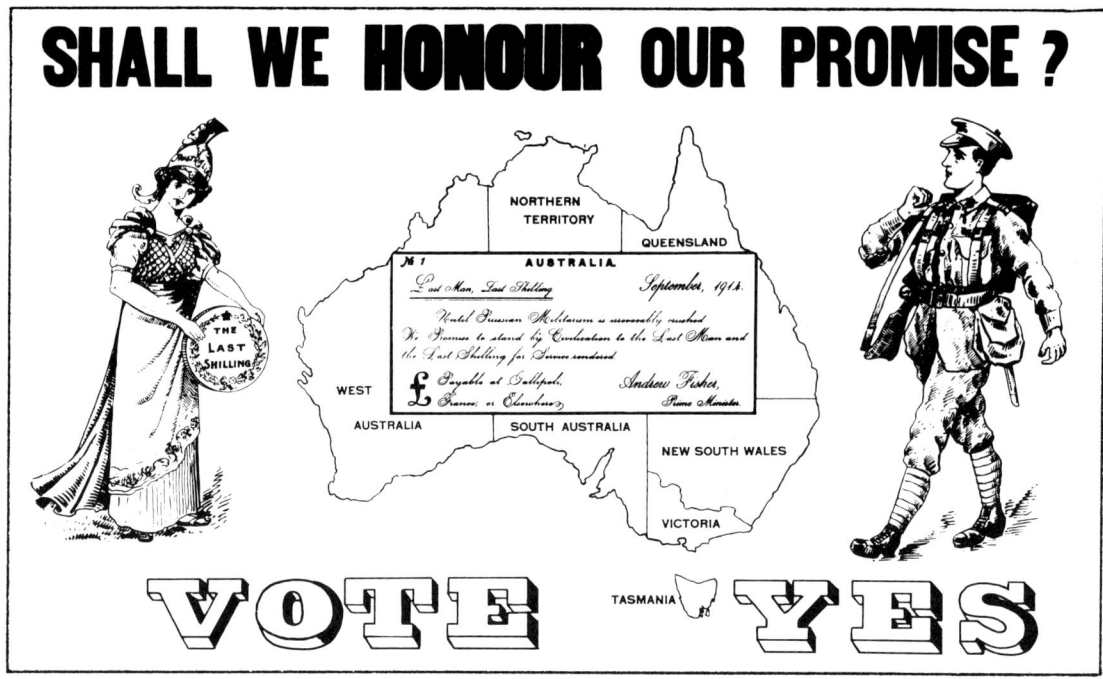

SHALL WE HONOUR OUR PROMISE ?

THE LAST SHILLING

№ 1   AUSTRALIA.

Last Man, Last Shilling   September, 1914.

Until Prussian Militarism is successfully crushed
We Promise to stand by Confederation to the Last Man and
the Last Shilling for Service rendered

£ Payable at Gallipoli,
France, or Elsewhere   Andrew Fisher,
Prime Minister

NORTHERN TERRITORY

QUEENSLAND

WEST AUSTRALIA

SOUTH AUSTRALIA

NEW SOUTH WALES

VICTORIA

TASMANIA

VOTE YES

Australian people were urged to vote 'yes' in favour of conscripting men for overseas service in the Great War. The promise so prominently featured here was that of Andrew Fisher, who became Labor prime minister in 1914.

In the Tasmanian parliament, Earle and one of his colleagues joined the Opposition in support of conscription, and J. A. Lyons became leader of the Labor party.

During the run-up to voting day (28 October 1916) the conscriptionists became increasingly hysterical, branding all opponents as German-lovers and worse, if that were possible. Catholics were suspected of disloyalty because they were usually of Irish origin and, as bigoted Protestants furiously asked, had not the Irish tried to stab England in the back after the Dublin Easter Rising.

Australia as a whole voted against conscription for overseas service, but Tasmania strongly favoured it, voting 49 493 to 37 833. The people were divided and embittered. The exploits of the Anzacs gave people a sense of pride and a focus for national feeling. The conscription issue destroyed it.

The Labor party split throughout Australia. In Tasmania a confused situation developed between the old Liberals and a new Win-the-War party or National Federation. Both groups detested Labor.

By-elections in the state confirmed the collapse of Labor support. By mid-1917 there were twenty government members in the House of Assembly and only ten Labor representatives.

The world seemed awash with the blood of warriors. Hatreds were redoubled during the Australian General Strike of August and September 1917. 'Loyalists' physically clashed with strikers at Devonport.

In their bewilderment, hysteria and fury at the huge losses on the Western Front, people rushed to extremes. Tensions were heightened by newspapers trumpeting news of 'victories' in France when, as a result of personal communications from the army, Tasmanians knew on the contrary that men were being killed and maimed by the thousand.

At the same time as Tasmania was tearing itself apart socially, politically and religiously, its sons in 1917 were again made victims of the mincing machine that was the Third Battle of Ypres. Here the AIF lost about 38 000 men, killed and wounded.

Hughes again begged the people to vote 'yes' in a conscription plebiscite, and again all hell broke loose. Issues similar to those of 1916 re-surfaced. The Tasmanian press, especially the *Mercury*, kept sectarianism on the boil by saying that Catholics were disloyal to the Empire.

Women anti-conscriptionists spoke out boldly and public meetings were rowdy. On 20 December 1917 the second plebiscite was held and Tasmania voted 38 881 for 'yes' and 38 502 for 'no'. This was an astonishingly different result to 1916 and appeared to be caused by many 1916 'yes' voters staying away from the polling booths.

As the war in Europe raged on—a sort of fire-storm which no one seemed able to control—some Tasmanians responded by forming Loyalty Leagues. These organizations swore to uphold the Empire, and carried within them elements of vicious anti-Catholicism and anti-Bolshevism.

After the Great War ended, this unusual hoarding used the defeat of Germany to encourage shopping at the first peace-time Christmas for four years. 'Der Tag' (The Day) was said to be a German toast to their expected victory over the Allies.

Side by side went another movement that continued to divide the people of Tasmania—prohibition. The supporters of this movement went further than mere temperance, advocating a complete embargo on the sale and distribution of alcohol.

Tasmania's agony and divisions were checked at last when, on 11 November 1918, Germany surrendered. The people in the island state gave themselves up to rejoicing and gloated about how much money the defeated enemy would be forced to pay in compensation.

Nothing socially constructive emerged from the greatest conflict in the history of the world. Of the 13 000 Tasmanians who had embarked, 2500 had been killed and many more returned home wounded in body and mind.

Questions for discussion

1   Explain the main social and political reforms instituted in Tasmania in the period c. 1901–14.

2   How and why was hydro-electricity developed in Tasmania?

3   What were the effects of the Great War on Tasmania 1914–18? Discuss life on the war fronts as it was experienced by the soldiers.

4   Why was Anzac Day made a public holiday in Tasmania? Do you think it will continue in its present form?

CHAPTER 6

The 1920s

I N THE STATE ELECTION OF 1919, the Nationalists won easily, securing seventeen seats to Labor's thirteen. But all was not well in the aftermath of war and the government failed to deliver the expected prosperity. In 1923 Labor returned to office and J. A. Lyons was premier for the next five years. During this period voting for the House of Assembly became compulsory by legislation of late 1924.

In 1925 a Tasmanian Rights League was formed to agitate for better shipping services. This highlighted one of the themes of the 1920s and beyond—the belief, growing into an article of faith, that Tasmanian business and tourism was hamstrung by poor shipping arrangements caused, it was said, by the Navigation Act. This Act passed by the federal government laid down conditions which made it uneconomic for shipping companies to offer the service Tasmanians wanted.

Soldier Settlement

What reward should be offered the returned heroes of the AIF? In response to a strong conviction that the volunteers must be rewarded and their sacrifices recognized, what became known as the soldier settlement scheme was introduced. The scheme was set in motion following a federal-states conference in Melbourne in 1916 and was based on the New Zealand example. An arrangement between the states and the federal government was worked out to pay for purchase of land, stock, seed, farm equipment and so on.

A few critics feared that there would be financial difficulties unless the returned soldier knew about farming but these people were disregarded in the atmosphere of general enthusiasm and patriotic fervour. As a result the states proceeded with the scheme too hurriedly and were confronted with a flood of applications from returning soldiers.

In Tasmania the soldier settlement scheme complemented and followed the Closer Settlement Act of 1906. Under this Act, commissioners bought and then sub-divided large land holdings, so that more people could become farmers.

The first purchase was 'Cheshunt', a property of 13 400 acres in the Deloraine district. It cost £48 000 and was split up into sixty-one farms. Numerous other properties were also sub-divided in the period leading up to the war, and by 1915 about 73 000 acres had been purchased by the government. Subsequently the work of the closer settlement board became largely concerned with placing soldiers on the land. By 1923 the state was divided into six sections, with the following number of soldier settlement properties:

Area	Number of soldier settlements	Total
1	Circular Head 87, Emu Bay 61, Table Cape 129, Penguin 47, Queenstown 1, Strahan 1	326
2	Deloraine 71, Devonport 17, Kentish 65, Latrobe 14, Leven 89, Westbury 29	285
3	Beaconsfield 39, George Town 16, Launceston 3, Lilydale 36, Longford 22, Ringarooma 47, Scottsdale 63, St Leonards 9, Portland 2	237
4	Bruny Island 16, Esperance 28, Huon 66, Kingborough 108, Port Cygnet 55	273
5	Brighton 39, Glamorgan 1, Oatlands 15, Richmond 62, Sorell 53, Tasman 9	179
6	Bothwell 4, Campbell Town 1, Clarence 19, Glenorchy 70, Green Ponds 15, Hamilton 15, New Norfolk 66, New Town/Hobart 11	201
	Flinders Island 12 King Island 71	83
	Total	1584

Inspectors were appointed for each of these areas, to assess how the men were getting on, and to help and advise them.

Some soldier settlers were able to struggle and finally make a decent living or at least break even. Others, however, were forced to desert their properties or succumbed to illnesss caused by their war experience. In an enquiry undertaken in 1926 evidence was given that more than £2 million had been spent on settling some 2000 Tasmanian and British returned soldiers. Out of that, the state had lost £720 000. By 1926 about 850 men remained on their blocks and it was forecast that no more than 500, with their families, would still be resident by 1928.

Why was this? The answer given by the board was that many of the settlers took to drink, destroyed their properties and were dishonest. With the failure of the scheme there were hints of political interference, some members of parliament advising the settlers not to repay their loans.

One of the major problems with the scheme was the initial failure to select applicants who had a reasonable chance of success. Some of the men were unfit for farming as a result of physical or mental war wounds, which in some cases they would never recover from. In addition, properties and stock were sometimes acquired at high prices and when the price of primary produce fell dramatically, settlers were hard hit and were unable to repay their loans. In response to these pressures a number of settlers simply walked off their farms, owing money which the government then had the difficult and distasteful task of getting back. Insurance officers became suspicious at the number of fires which destroyed buildings.

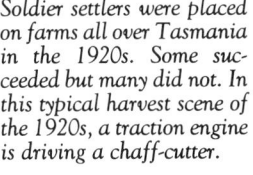

Soldier settlers were placed on farms all over Tasmania in the 1920s. Some succeeded but many did not. In this typical harvest scene of the 1920s, a traction engine is driving a chaff-cutter.

Much of the hardship caused by the soldier settlement scheme was borne by the wives and families of the returned men. Those who stuck to their properties found, or already knew only too well, that hard physical work was the keynote to life on the land.

Primary Industry

Tractors were still virtually non-existent in Tasmania. Apart from shearing machines, about the only form of modern agricultural machinery was the traction engine, which travelled the country threshing cereal crops and cutting chaff. Harvesting machines were pulled by horses.

The fruit crops were picked by hand and, although in 1920 a new hop-picking machine was installed on a property in the Derwent Valley, hops too were harvested manually by seasonal workers. A certain amount of seasonal labour was also employed in timber-getting and associated industries such as saw-milling.

The timber industry was distinguished by lack of central control. Trees appeared to some people like the fish in the sea— ever renewable and always there for the taking. This was not quite true. As the rare and valuable whales and seals were 'harvested' to extinction, or the edge of it, so were certain types of Tasmanian timber. Indeed the very word 'harvest' was misleading because it supposed a renewable resource under control of the harvesters, who should also have been planters. They were not.

The history of the management of forestry resources in Tasmania was characterized by inaction. Until 1881 there were no government arrangements for conservation of Tasmania's huge timber resources on crown land. Then an Act of Parliament made provision for land to be set aside for preservation and growth of timber.

Four years later the State Forest Act authorized the appointment of a conservator. Following this the government introduced the idea of a timber royalty, whereby those felling trees for profit paid the government a small fee.

Control of this was left to the police, who were already over-burdened and under-paid. Timber-getting continued undiminished and the bush was exploited illegally. Then in 1898 exclusive cutting rights for sawmillers were introduced in the form of a lease and royalty payment. Again, this was difficult to police and manage, for in remote areas, no one took much notice of illegal tree felling, even if they knew such activity existed.

At an inter-state conference on forestry in April 1920 held in Hobart speakers condemned Tasmania for its poor management of forests. Representatives from other states were astonished at the extensive area granted by Tasmanian governments to sawmillers under conditions that placed large powers of control and long-term leases in private hands.

Visitors drew attention to the Esperance and Cygnet area where timber was being taken without proper method so that the

The nature and importance of the Tasmanian bush made expert axemen invaluable from the time of first settlement of the island. Carnivals such as this were part of the social scene in Tasmania.

PLEASE POST UP.

Australian
Axemen's Carnival
(REGISTERED)

ULVERSTONE, TASMANIA
November 25th and 26th, 1927

Patron—His Excellency Lord Stonehaven, Governor-General of Australia.

Vice-Patrons—His Excellency Admiral Sir Dudley de Chair, K.C.B., Governor of New South Wales.
His Excellency Sir William Compson, K.C.M.G., Governor of Western Australia.
His Excellency Sir James O'Grady, K.C.M.G., Governor of Tasmania.

Lieut.-Governor of Queensland (Hon. William Lennon).
Hon. J. A. Lyons, M.H.A., Premier of Tasmania.
President—Dr. F. A. Ferris.
Chairman—Capt. C. Roger Jones.
Manager—Hon. H. A. Nichols.
Asst. Secretary—E. F. Plummer, Esq.

PROGRAMME.

1. HOPETOUN CUP—Prizes £130 (World's Championship Chop). Standing Blocks, 4ft. girth. Prizes : First, Cup and Gold Medal given by Plumb Axe Co., U.S.A., with £50 added, and Optional Special of £11 ; second, £15; third, £7; fourth, £3. Others in Final, Trophy or £1 each.

2. BRADDON CUP—Of £50. Double-Handed Sawing Championship. First prize, two Gold Medals, £15; second, £6; third, £3; fourth, £2.

3. HAMILTON CUP—Prizes £40. Underhand Championship, 4ft. girth Logs. First, Cup and £12; second, £3; third, £2; fourth, £1. Others in Final £1 each.

4. TASMANIAN CENTENARY CUP—Of £250. Handicap Standing Blocks, 4ft. girth. First prize, Cup, with £100 added, Gold Medal value £5/5/ given by E. Keen Esq., and optional Special Prize of £30; second, £30; third, £15; fourth, £8; fifth, £4. Others in final divide £10.

5. HENRY CUP—Prizes £40. World's Champion S.H. Sawing. First prize, Cup, Gold Medal and £15; second, £6; third, £3; fourth, £2. Others in final Trophy or £1 each.

6. PETTIT COMPETITION—Of £45. D.H. Handicap Sawing. First prize, Trophies and £20; second, £7; third, £5; fourth, £2. Others in Final, Trophy or £1 each.

7. ATKINSON HANDICAP—of £40. Handicap S.H. Sawing. First prize, Gold Medal, Trophy, and £12 ; second, £6 ; third, £3. Others in Final, £1 each.

8. REEVES HANDICAP STAKES—of £70. 12in. Standing Blocks. First prize, Trophy and £25, with Optional Special of £15; second, £10; third, £5; fourth, £2. Others in Final, Trophy or £1 each.

9. LYONS HANDICAP—of £50. Handicap Underhand Chop, 4ft. girth Logs. First prize, Cup, with £12 added, and optional Special Prize of £10; second, £5; third, £3; fourth, £2. Others in Final divide £5.

(Under Authority of Ulverstone Athletic Club.)

10. HANDICAP MILE RACE—of £115. First, £50, with two Optional Specials of £20 each; second, £10; third, £5. Others in Final divide £10. Nomination, 20/-; acceptance, 5/-; optional acceptance each £1.

11. HALF-MILE HANDICAP—of £35... First, £12, with Optional Special of £10; second, £5; third, £3. Others in Final divide £5. Nomination, 7/6; acceptance, 5/-; optional acceptance, 10/-

12. TUG-OF-WAR (8 men aside), prize, £20. Entry, 5/- per man. Four entries or prize reduced.

SPECIAL FARES ON RAILWAYS.   ALL EVENTS, IF NECESSARY, WILL BE DECIDED IN HEATS.

Special Allowance to Non-winning Competitors from distant parts of Australia and New Zealand.

OPTIONAL ACCEPTANCE FEES may be paid up till Three Days before the event.   Payment of such fees alone entitles the Winner to Optional Prizes.

All Sawing Event Logs 5ft. girth.   All Competitors Pay Admission to the Ground.

NOMINATIONS (with performances) close on OCTOBER 17.

NOMINATIONS AS FOLLOWS :

	Nom.	Accept.	Optional Accept.		Nom.	Accept.	Optional Accept.		Nom.	Accept.	Optional Accept.
Event No. 1	20/-	10/-	20/-	Event No. 4	30/-	10/-	40/-	Event No. 7	10/-	5/-	—
Event No. 2	15/-	5/-	—	Event No. 5	15/-	5/-	—	Event No. 8	15/-	5/-	20/-
Event No. 3	15/-	5/-	—	Event No. 6	15/-	5/-	—	Event No. 9	10/-	5/-	20/-

H. A. NICHOLS, Manager, Ulverstone, Tasmania.

"Chronicle" Print

COME TO TASMANIA—THE WONDERLAND.

Two axemen have stepped around this tree for the photograph. Cut branches were used for the main supports for the platform on which the men stand and cut. It was most important to cut the 'scarf' so that the falling tree did not lodge on another tree.

surviving bush was left ruined. On the north-west coast, it appeared that government inaction had nearly led to the destruction of the beautiful and valuable blackwood trees.

There was a conflict between those who thought of tomorrow's resources and the environment, and those who thought largely in terms of their own pockets and immediate profit and employment.

Following the conference, the Forestry Act of 1921 established a Department of Forestry to do something about indiscriminate timber-getting. It was, however, getting late to implement a coherent policy of forest management and for many years this important natural resource was to suffer at the hands of the short-sighted and the greedy.

Wool production continued as the chief mainstay of the Tasmanian economy. In 1924 it was calculated that the most valuable products of the soil during the preceding ten years were wool: £6.5m., hay: £6m., potatoes: £5.3m., dairying: £5.2m., apples: £4.5m., pears: £0.5m.

Mineral production also remained important and a new find, osmiridium, was exploited during the period. By 1920 about 250 men were employed in the area between Mount Jasper and the Savage River. The industry indirectly attracted publicity, following the great success of *Jewelled Nights*, a book about the area by the romantic novelist, Marie Bjelke-Petersen. In 1925 a film, based on the novel, was made, starring Miss Louise Lovely.

Apples were the glamour industry of Tasmania, largely because the industry linked the state closely to Great Britain. Tasmanian fruit filled the off-season gap during the northern spring and summer. Exports from Hobart were at their height in mid-May each year, and large quantities exported. In 1914 950 000 cases of fruit were sent out of the state, 460 000 in 1920, 1.35m. in 1922, 1.5m. in 1923 and more than 2m. cases in 1926.

Secondary Industry

Cheap hydro-electricity was the magnet which the Tasmanian government persisted in hoping would successfully attract secondary industry to the state in the 1920s.

By itself, however, hydro-electricity was not enough. The climate also had to be suitable for the industry concerned and it was desirable to have easy access to a good deep-water port. Even more important in the pre-automation age was a supply of reliable, docile labour and the presence of the raw material to be manufactured.

The Electrolytic Zinc Company was well suited in terms of all these requirements, which outweighed the disadvantages of isolation.

Another industry that established itself in Tasmania at this time was Cadbury-Fry-Pascall of England (later Cadbury Schweppes Australia). In 1920 the company secured an option over 246 acres at Claremont, near Hobart, with the aim of manufacturing confectionery and food drinks such as cocoa. The directors saw the area as ideal because there was electric power and a source of labour readily available. An additional factor was the temperate climate, known to be excellent for the manufacture of chocolates. By September 1921 what was termed a 'garden village' was being established at Claremont, and 'Chigwell' had been purchased as a temporary hostel for expert women workers brought from England. A year later the manufacture of sweets started, though the factory was not yet quite finished.

Women wrapping chocolates at the factory owned by Cadbury-Fry-Pascall at Claremont, near Hobart.

At the same time the Electrolytic Zinc Company continued to expand. In 1920 the west-coast Hercules and Rosebery mines were bought. In 1923, with the recent completion of the Waddamana power station, the company produced 100 tons of zinc a day. The following year it began manufacturing superphosphate and by 1927 annual production at the works ran to 49 000 tons. Zinc concentrate came from Broken Hill and from the Rosebery mines. For a time the west-coast ore was shipped to Risdon via Strahan but in 1924 work was conducted at Zeehan, where the necessary plant was built. It operated till 1930, when the Depression led to the closure of nearly all operations on the west coast.

Another enterprise which emerged in the state during the 1920s was the Goliath Portland Cement Company. From 1926 this business set out to make cement from limestone deposits in the Railton district. First annual output was 25 000 tons from Tasmanian Cement Pty Ltd, taken over in 1928. By the end of the 1920s, new kiln capacity enabled production of 65 000 tons a year.

The new resource of electric power was also put to work by the Waverley Woollen Mills at Launceston. This company first manufactured woollen goods on hand-looms at Distillery Creek as early as 1874, with waterwheel power originally derived from piped water.

Hydro-electric power was also used by the textile manufacturers, Kelsall and Kemp. The English directors of this company visited Tasmania after the Great War and in 1921 building started on the Launceston factory. Two years later production was under way of flannels, suitings and tweeds, and later blankets.

Similarly, Patons and Baldwins (later Coats Patons Australia) were attracted from their English base to Glen Dhu, Launceston, because of the availability of a suitable labour force and the area's cool temperature, humid air, cheap electricity and soft water. Work on this site began in 1922 and it was fully established a year later. Business was so good that, ten years after its start, the factory floor expanded by 50 per cent.

Population

On the surface, then, Tasmania appeared to be prosperous in these years of the 1920s. Certainly there were more opportunities for employment in the cities and the extension of electricity supplies was a great benefit.

On the other hand, the newspapers were full of complaints that Tasmania was overlooked by the federal government and the more opulent states of Australia.

Tasmania was extremely vulnerable to shipping strikes. Howls of anguish arose when the tourist trade was thereby thought to be ruined, and commerce disrupted.

During the 1920s governments and experts became concerned that the state was being left behind the others in population growth, if not in industrialization. Censuses reveal that the population of Tasmania increased from 171 703 (1901), 188 570 (1911), 212 008 (1921) to 227 599 (1933). These figures were certainly considerably below those expected if Tasmania had kept with Australia as a whole. The average annual rate of population increase in Australia 1901–11 was 1.67 per cent (Tasmania 1.04), 1911–21, 2.01 (Tasmania 1.12), 1921–33, 1.63 (Tasmania 0.52).

The slow rate of increase in population was largely due to emigration of Tasmanians to the mainland, a phenomenon common to all similar parts of the world. It could have been argued that a slow rate of population increase was in fact better than a fast one which might overtax facilities, but no one held that view. Tasmanians were sensitive to criticism, conscious of their tiny size in the Australian context, and continued to yearn to 'develop' the state and massively increase the number of people in it.

In addition, Tasmania sought to share in the federal government's 'men, money and markets' plan. Australia was to advance, according to this theory, by attracting immigrants ('men'—and women) from Britain, by accepting loans from Britain ('money'), and by selling Australian produce in Britain ('markets'). This was the customary role of Australia as a colony and Tasmania of course was part of the grand design. As part of the plan immigrants were to come from Britain. To this end an immigration officer was appointed in 1921. In 1922 some 700 immigrants arrived in Tasmania, 290 in 1923 and 238 in 1924. It was scarcely a flood and the newcomers did not compensate for emigration. From 1921–5 there was an annual loss to the state of 3500 people which natural increase was failing to overtake.

In 1926 the birth rate was 23.5 compared to 24.5 the preceding year, and so the lowest since 1850. This was a decline since 1913 of more than 20 per cent. The rate of natural increase was also down from 15.1 persons a thousand in 1925 to 14.5 in 1926. Yet the natural increase in Tasmania remained higher than in any other state, despite the fact that the marriage rate at 6.76 was the lowest since 1918.

These figures were interpreted by government and experts to mean that the loss of people from the state was a cause for great alarm. On the contrary, for the people concerned, it clearly represented the prospect of better employment on the mainland or, to put it another way, lack of employment opportunities at home.

More to the point was whether the standard of living of Tasmanians was increasing. The descriptive evidence, especially the advance of electrification, suggests that it was. During the 1920s thousands of Tasmanians came to enjoy the comfort and convenience of electric light and appliances and marvelled how they had ever done without it. Launceston was connected in 1922 and other areas such as the north-west in 1926 and 1927, the only complaint made against the spread of electric power lines being a quaint belief that they drew moisture from the air and thus were the cause of dry weather.

Extensive new housing was built in Hobart and Launceston in 1923 and 1924, after investigations into living conditions during the Spanish influenza pandemic of 1919 revealed a disgraceful state of affairs.

The flu, together with strikes on the waterfront and among maritime unions, interrupted the tourist trade, but by 1926 all passenger traffic records were broken when 60 152 persons crossed Bass Strait. It is not clear how many people were going in which direction.

Transport

The 1920s is frequently termed the 'Roaring Twenties' or the 'Jazz Age', terms which conjure up pictures of free-swinging entertainment, Dixieland jazz, low-slung racing cars and barn-storming aeroplanes.

The Great War gave an enormous impetus to aircraft production and design. In the 1920s the airways of the world were nearly all pioneered and conquered, though aviation still remained a hazardous business.

Out on the edge of the world, Tasmanians took a special interest in aviation. The challenge of flying across Bass Strait particularly encouraged aviators as well as those interested in air travel for commerce or defence.

The first commercial flight in Tasmania came on 27 October 1919, five years after the first aeroplane flight in the state, when Lieutenant Arthur Long made a return journey from Hobart to Launceston, stopping at Deloraine. He dropped souvenir copies of the *Mercury* and delivered papers at Launceston and Deloraine.

On 16 December of the same year, Long flew from Stanley to Port Melbourne in just under five hours, the first air flight over Bass Strait. The first flight from Flinders Island to Tasmania was in July 1921 and in September of that year the first air trip from Launceston to Welshpool in Victoria took place. In 1924 a return flight was made from Melbourne to Hobart and three years later Tasmania Air Services was formed by the Holyman family.

Preoccupation with 'development' in the 1880s and beyond led to extensive construction of railways, which were enthusiastically supported by colonists who concluded that they would be of great economic benefit to the districts concerned.

In the 1920s the growth of road transport revealed the weaknesses of the railway system. All over Australia competition between rail and road transport, in terms of freight and numbers of people passengers carried, suddenly became apparent. The rail system was publicly (government) owned and thus people began to suggest that the government should tax road users to save the railway system, especially passenger lines. Too frequently in Tasmania railways were laid down to satisfy some local demand or fancy without looking carefully enough into the economics of the matter.

Argument arose about what was 'economic'. In theory, low railway freight and passenger charges would, or might, keep down road freight charges but this in turn was difficult to sell to road interests and the booming motor production industry. In addition there was heavy advertising involved in the sale of cars, trucks and motor bikes, so people were encouraged to buy their own form of private, modern and smart transport.

Essentially, the attack on the public transport system came from two quarters—private people buying their own motor cars and private companies urging the public to use motor buses.

Hobart and Launceston councils responded by creating their own fleets of buses but the move to private motorized transport became irresistible. A Launceston–Burnie daily motor service started in mid–1923, and in the same year the triumph and excitement of the motor car was exhibited when, on 29 September, two

This is an early Launceston bus ('No. 2'), with driver and ticket collector, and one passenger. The increasing popularity of private motor cars led Launceston and Hobart councils to augment their tramway services with fleets of city buses in order to compete.
(right)

The coming of the motor car and motor traffic was a mixed blessing. A privately-owned car or motorbike was an exciting novelty. It changed many lives, but not always for the better, as seen here in the beginning of an increasingly serious road toll.

MOTORING ACCIDENTS

A Youth Run Over

Severe Head Injuries

Severe injuries were received by Valentine Conrades, aged 16 years, who resides at Birch's Bay, as the result of being run over by a motor-car yesterday. When Mr. Albert Nicholls was driving his car along the Birch's Bay-Woodbridge Road he noticed four youths near a bend. Two ran to one side of the road and their companions to the other. As the car approached, it is said, Conrades and another of the youths commenced to run alongside of the road, and when the car was only a few yards in the rear Conrades crossed in front. The car did not have time to pull up, and Conrades was knocked down and the car passed over him.

The injured youth was conveyed to the Hobart Public Hospital, and it was ascertained that he had probably received fracture of the skull and fracture of the left shoulder. There were also abrasions on his face. His condition last night was critical.

TRAFFIC OFFICER INJURED.

Traffic Patrol Officer Thomas Males, aged 26 years, was proceeding on a motor-cycle along the Main Road, New Town, shortly after 6 o'clock on Saturday evening in company with Constable Westall, who was in the side-car, when, trying to get the motor-cycle moving, after having pulled up at a bowser for petrol, Males was using the kick starter when a motor-omnibus going in the same direction struck the cycle a glancing blow.

Males received a sprained ankle, and also was suffering from shock when admitted to the Public Hospital. Constable Westall was not injured, and only slight damage was done to the motor-cycle.

A CITY COLLISION.

A collision occurred last evening at the intersection of Argyle and Liverpool Streets between a double-seater motor-car, driven by Lewis Hickman, of Margate, and a motor-cycle, ridden by Arthur Alomes, of Sorell, who had as a passenger on the pillion seat Eric Sweet, of New Town. Hickman was driving up Liverpool Street, in the direction of Elizabeth Street, and Alomes was going up Argyle Street, in the direction of New Town. At the intersection the motor-cycle struck the car, and Sweet was thrown to the ground. He was taken to the Public Hospital, where it was found he was suffering only from abrasions to the face. Hickman and Alomes escaped without injuries, and neither vehicle was much damaged.

COLLISION AT GRANTON.

men in a car drove from Launceston to Hobart in only two hours and thirty-nine minutes.

Already road accidents had occurred. On 5 April 1924 the mail bus running between St Helens and St Marys fell into the Scamander River and nine passengers were rescued by boat.

Motoring swiftly began changing the lifestyle of Tasmanians. Motorized police units were established in Hobart and Launceston and, in the interests of the motor trade, the government set about mapping the state road system. They termed it 'charting' to indicate that dangerous features and gradients were clearly shown.

A table of distances was also planned, so that motorists might calculate their journeys more accurately, and not be forced to depend on locals offering estimates of how far it was to a certain place, along with unique descriptions of the landmarks to be encountered and used as guides on the way.

Increase in motor ownership and use led to more and substantial expenditure on the upkeep and construction of roads, on which much of the 'money' of the government's 'men, money and markets' was spent. Given the terrain of Tasmania, this could be expensive indeed, but the pressure was such that even a road from Hobart to Queenstown, through most inhospitable and difficult country, was completed by 1932.

New houses were now built on blocks of land large enough to contain the all-important garage by the side of the dwelling. Service stations, repair works and many other industries spun off from the thrusting force of the motor vehicle.

The growth in car ownership had social effects too. Glamour and prestige were attached to ownership of a car. People were able to travel more readily, though probably less cheaply, than they could by rail, and they had no need to worry about missing their train or consulting time-tables.

The police found they had ever-increasing duties in relation to the new form of transport. Vehicles had to be registered and as the numbers increased rapidly, the government found itself with a very handy source of revenue. Special speed limits were imposed and more and more rules of the road were framed and enforced.

The first police car in Tasmania was a chain-driven Talbot machine, transferred from the Premier's Department in the mid-1920s. Little use, however, was made of police cars in the state until about 1940.

In 1919 a Hobart sergeant of police was appointed to supervise traffic control and the following year the control of all metropolitan traffic was put in the hands of the police department.

The 1920s was a decade of motor travel, with massive government expenditure on roads, and house blocks wide enough to accommodate a garage. Motor bikes were cheaper to buy than cars. This 1925 BSA machine is complete with a 'pedestrian-slicer' front number plate.

Collection: TASMANIAN MUSEUM AND ART GALLERY

(detail)

So was signalled the end of an era. Horse-drawn vehicles were doomed, though they were still often to be met with on Tasmanian roads right through until the end of the 1930s.

Cultural Change

Gramophones became common. A dance craze swept through society and conservative people feared that youth was hell-bent on its own destruction. In 1926 Ulverstone Council saw danger ahead and forbade the dancing of the Charleston within the boundaries of the municipality. Open air palais-de-danses proliferated.

American films swamped the Australian-made ones, which became increasingly rare during the period, in the face of Hollywood's technical excellence and advertising, as well as the American takeover of film distribution.

Tasmanians became keen film-goers and in 1921 a Hobart church deputation asked the mayor to take immediate action to prevent films being shown on a Sunday.

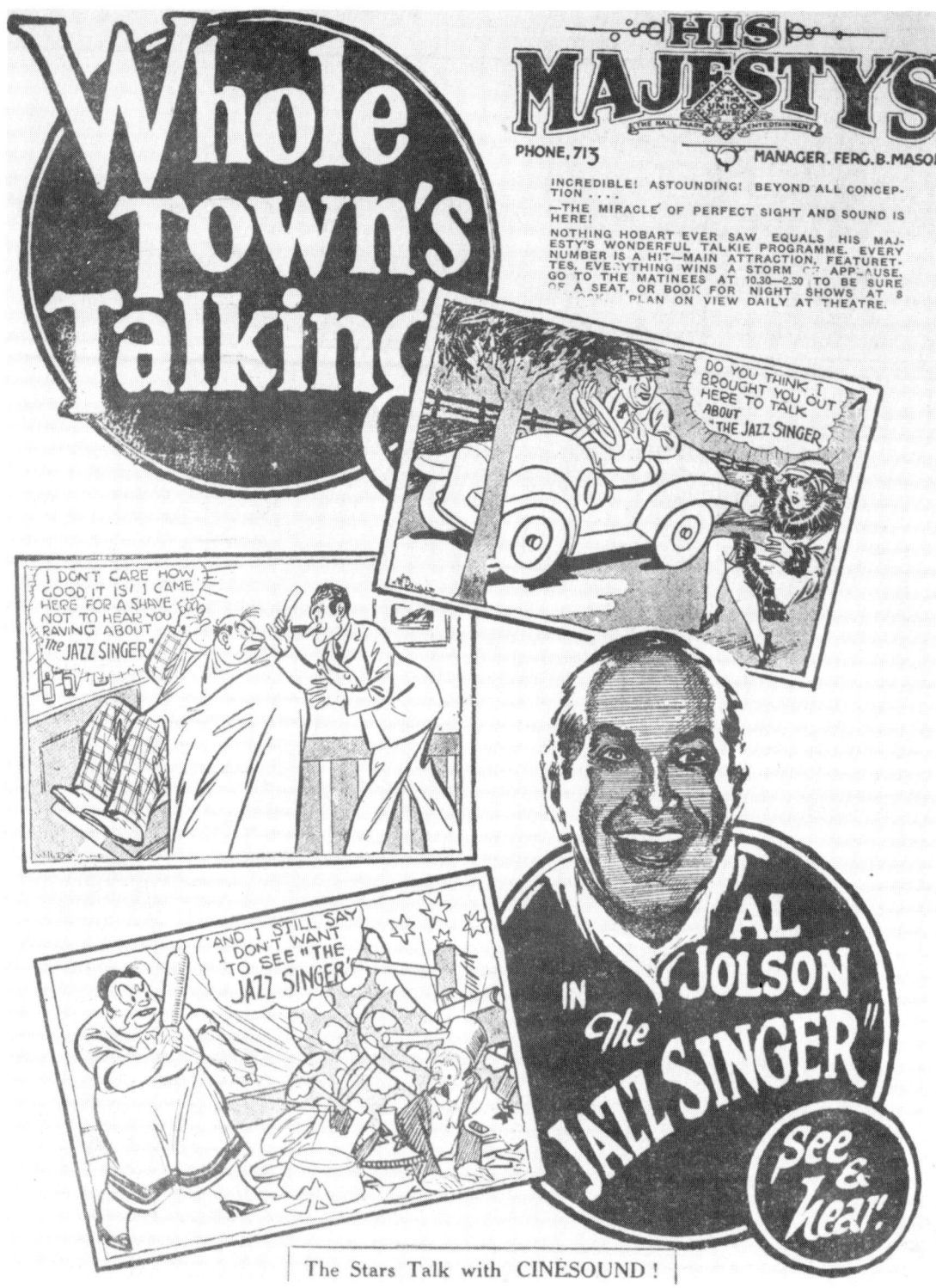

The Stars Talk with CINESOUND!

The invention of synchron-
ized sound made the silent
movies into 'talkies' in
1929. Despite the economic
depression and the high cost
of admission, Tasmanians
remained enthusiastic film-
goers.

(opposite)

No such objections were made against another wonder of the age—wireless. One of the first 'stations' was established in 1925 by the Associated Radio Company of Australia at the office of the *Mercury*. People with technical skill began manufacturing sets to receive primitive local broadcasting and by the beginning of March 1927 there were more than 2000 wireless licence holders in the state.

For a time sets were 'sealed' so that the listener could hear only one station but ingenious people quickly bypassed this constraint. Then 'A' and 'B' class stations came into existence, the former bringing in government revenue, the latter destined to become the commercial stations. In Hobart 7ZL became an 'A' station in late 1927.

During this period women came to be perceived in quite different terms from their mothers or grandmothers. Although women were not 'liberated' in the sense that was to become known sixty years later, some began to enjoy a more satisfying and challenging role. Increased opportunities for employment created what was known for a while as 'the new woman' of 1919–20. She was never clearly defined but was rather more dignified than the 'flapper'. Doubts about the origin of this word reflect the sense of excitement and turmoil for young women and teenage girls during this period.

The use of makeup became common, hair was bobbed and hemlines rose. Lighter fabrics were introduced, greatly decreasing the weight of women's clothes and permitting more freedom of movement.

A number of political advances took place during this period. The year 1922 turned out to be a turning point—women were permitted to stand for parliament; a women's deputation to the attorney-general learnt that he would recommend to cabinet that women be appointed as Justices of the Peace; the first female dentist began in the profession and two women candidates stood for parliament, one of them Mrs Enid Lyons, wife of the Labor leader.

Earlier that year the Tasmanian Women's Non-Party Political League was formed with the aim of putting candidates forward to try to obtain full civil rights for women and to improve conditions in education and public health, to obtain a firmer consideration of social questions and immediately to press for the bringing into force of the Mental Deficiency Act. The first all-female club, the Quamby Club, was formed at Launceston in 1923. The following year the government lived up to its promise and appointed women Justices of the Peace. In 1927 the government sought to provide for the regulation of trained nurses and control of their calling, with provision for a Nurses' Registration Board and reciprocity with other states. The government thereby gave recognition to and enhanced the standing of an important occupation for women.

She has no Picnic Worry . . . .

This idealized 'housewife', by purchasing Arnott's biscuits, is said to be helping the Tasmanian wheat industry, and escaping from 'kitchen drudgery'.

Nevertheless, women still received less pay for the work they did than men, even where they were doing exactly the same job. The role of women remained essentially that of second-class citizens in a strongly male-dominated society, which differed little in its perception of women's role from colonial society. Still, events such as the founding of the state high schools certainly enabled young women to glimpse a wider horizon and contemplate opportunities other than marriage and the raising of children.

Women had been touched by the edges of the Jazz Age and its excitement, but it was typical that civic and business interests eagerly encouraged such events as beauty contests in 1927.

There is no convincing evidence that standards of morality changed seriously in the Roaring Twenties. Sex education in any meaningful sense did not exist and young women's knowledge of their own bodies remained, in many cases, tragically limited. Tasmania, like most of Australia, remained a puritanical and prudish place, suspicious of outside influences, largely ignorant of the rest of the world and proud to be British.

How did the rest of the world see Tasmania? Most other Australians knew the island state as a tourist resort and there were some, such as the novelist Martin Boyd, who made regular visits during the summer months. Some knew a little about the state as the result of reading novels such as those by Roy Bridges. Tattersalls Lotteries were known far and wide to be based in Hobart. Movies such as *For the Term of his Natural Life*, re-made in 1926 with no expense spared, publicized an aspect of Tasmania which some Tasmanians would have preferred to forget.

The voyage to the state and back to the mainland was always featured as a thrilling journey to a beautiful island with excellent fishing, boating, hiking and so on, not to mention the largest historical ruins in Australia at Port Arthur.

However, the passage across Bass Strait, well-known as an ugly piece of water, could be frightful. If storms blew up, as they frequently did, the small vessels plying the Strait came in for a rough time. So did their passengers. Accommodation for most sea travellers left a good deal to be desired, and many and varied were the suggested ways to avoid seasickness. It was said that some of the Bass Strait steamers would roll even on wet grass.

Accommodation in the island was criticized. Good hotels and guest houses were few and far between. Those who conducted them as summer enterprises did their best, but were perhaps not very up-to-date in their approach to the business of tourism. Too often the attitude was 'take it or leave it'.

For most tourists Tasmania's scenic beauty and temperate climate was attraction enough, despite the fact that the weather could be extremely unpredictable. Snow was known to fall on Mount Wellington at Christmas; the weather in the high country was extremely treacherous and dangerous to the uninitiated; and in 1929 disastrous floods occurred at Launceston.

That was of little consequence, however, in relation to what was happening on the international front. Export prices dropped by half in 1928 and unemployment increased sharply in Tasmania. The glitter that had characterized the 1920s was replaced by gloom, fear and, for many, a decade of grinding hardship and demoralization.

Questions for discussion

1 What was the soldier settlement scheme and to what extent did it succeed in its aims?

2 What were the state's main secondary industries in the 1920s? Why were they established in Tasmania? What was the day-to-day work routine?

3 How and why was the development of motor transport a cause of both concern and pleasure to governments and people?

4 Did the role of women change significantly in the period 1919–29?

5 What forms of education were offered?

Note: For all the above questions, students are advised to talk with people who recall the period.

CHAPTER 7

The Great Depression

I N THE LATE 1920s the prices of Australia's main exports, such as wool and wheat, fell. The stock market on Wall Street, New York, crashed catastrophically, heralding a crisis of confidence in the business world. Australia found it could no longer borrow money as it had done so easily during the 1920s. Overseas lenders demanded that interest payments on loans be paid forthwith and refused to convert existing loans for new loans. The immediate result of dwindling export prices and the drying up of funds was massive unemployment.

While Australia had suffered an economic depression in the 1890s the depression of the 1930s was on a far vaster scale. No one was quite sure why these terrible things were happening. Some spoke of an international conspiracy and others hopelessly concluded that God had spoken.

One of the problems had been created by optimism in the preceding decade when Tasmania, like other states, borrowed money in what was now perceived to be a reckless manner. Interest repayments were to have been financed by continuing growth, but when the export market plummeted, the government was faced with the frightening problem of having to earmark a great deal of its dwindling revenue for repayment of those debts.

Meetings of the state premiers with the federal government were held, and the opinion of experts sought on what to do in this desperate situation. In Canberra, seat of the federal government since the move from Melbourne in 1927, conflict and disharmony occurred in the ranks of the Scullin Labor government elected in 1929.

In 1929 Joseph Lyons, the premier of Tasmania for much of the 1920s, was persuaded to enter federal politics as a Labor member. Upheavals in that party led to the Scullin government's defeat when Lyons and a few others, after agonizing conflict of emotion and ideology, decided to resign from the party and lead a new United Australia Party. The UAP won a convincing victory at the polls.

J. A. Lyons (1879–1939) was a school teacher before becoming a member of parliament; subsequently he became premier of Tasmania, and then prime minister of Australia from 1932 until his death in 1939. During his career in Tasmania, he sought political and social consensus, and gained a reputation as a skilful financial manager.

Attempted Remedies

Sir Otto Niemeyer, a representative of Australia's creditors in London, journeyed to Australia as head of an inspection team from the Bank of England. He toured the nation and finally advised the government and people to tighten belts and cut costs in all directions.

The recommendation was accepted and there was a 10 per cent reduction in the federal basic wage. Following Niemeyer's visit the Premiers' Plan, with its proposal to reduce government spending and wait for better times, was agreed upon and introduced by the states.

Despite the forcibly-expressed opinion of J. T. Lang (the Labor premier of New South Wales) and his followers, that Australia should cease repayments to Britain during the crisis, the Australian people and governments in general did what they were told to do by London and entered upon a period of great hardship.

Lang's idea of temporarily suspending interest payments was greeted with horror, as was another suggestion that the currency be slightly inflated so that money for employment could be created. Despite the scale of the crisis, nothing unorthodox or adventurous was tried.

At this time there were no unemployment benefits on a national or state basis. It is important to grasp that the many champions of states rights and supporters of the idea that people had to stand on their own feet no matter what, saw the federal government as a distant force, usually the first to be called upon for help if business was threatened, but deeply distrusted at any other time.

In Tasmania, where unemployment in the 1920s had averaged about 10 per cent anyway, those out of work had traditionally been assisted by friends and relatives, become objects of charity to individuals and private organizations, or survived by begging and wandering around doing odd jobs.

Now the problem was monstrous and quite beyond the traditional means of relieving distress. A great strain was thrown on the government of the state but what could it do? One thing it could do was to try to get grants from Canberra, and indeed some funds were forthcoming. In turn, this money was handed over to unemployment councils or local bodies but there was simply not the money available on the scale needed nor, importantly, the actual machinery to administer relief schemes on such a vast scale.

Unemployment Relief

There was a desperate need to create work and to ensure that the unemployed got something to eat and somewhere to shelter. Fearing that a revolutionary situation might develop, some people also felt the pressing need to keep the unemployed under control.

A scheme whereby shopkeepers accepted a printed form issued to the deserving by government agencies enabled the victims of the Depression to claim sustenance (the 'susso'). The 'susso' entitled the person concerned to receive rations of bread, meat and so on, with the government footing the bill when the shopkeeper sent in an account.

There was also the dole, a loosely used term that could include vouchers for food or clothes, employment on public works or small amounts of money. The dole was administered differently in different states and the overall picture was one of confusion and ad hoc arrangements. For the person out of work and with few or no resources or savings it mattered little what name was given to the various schemes.

The typical unemployment relief in Tasmania was privately-organized by groups such as Rotary and Toc H. The new Labor government elected in 1934, however, did increase sustenance and work for the dole rates by 20 per cent in the cities and 30 per cent in rural areas.

Unemployed workers on the Risdon–Old Beach Road, January 1932.

Some of the unemployed banded together in the Unemployed Workers' Movement to bring pressure on employers and government. Although organizations such as the UWM and the few members of the Communist Party threw some Tasmanians into a frenzy of fear, and indeed won some victories, a feature of the Depression was the lack of effective high-level political action.

The people were told that the Depression was quite beyond immediate solution, and largely rejected radicalism. Tasmanians gave the impression of simply knuckling down until the worst was over. By 1931–2 at least one-third of the work force and probably more, was out of work. The blow fell most severely on those dependent on such industries as the building trades, and the winter of 1933 was a bad time indeed.

In July of that year the government of the state, supported by the Rotary and Toc H Clubs, launched an appeal for the unemployed, dubbed 'A Tasmanian Plan for Tasmanian Men and Women'. 'Will you help to provide work?' was the theme question.

J. C. McPhee, the Premier, commended the appeal. The objective was to provide, both in the city and country, as much work as possible during the winter months when unemployment usually reached its peak. The appeal sought to find employment for citizens who were out of work, and to keep in work some of those who might be in danger of losing it.

The logic of this appeal was that those in a position to spend money wisely should do so because the purchase of goods meant depletion of stocks. Depletion of stocks meant replenishment and replenishment created employment. It was a good time to buy, urged the Premier, because prices were low and low prices appealed to the thrifty buyer.

Behind this message lay an appeal to spend as the way out of the Depression. It did not work because individuals did not have nearly enough spending power—only governments and large businesses did.

Anyone who could offer direct employment, it was stated, had a clear responsibility in that time of anxiety, and those who provided work would be rendering a public service, the value of which could hardly be over-estimated.

There was a telling air of desperation, as well as repetition, in the appeal. The plan would not cure unemployment in Tasmania or anywhere else, it admitted, but it would help. Very many Tasmanians, continued the appeal, had to face a workless winter and only those who had been through it would know the tragedy of that. Others who had been more fortunate were having a bright and cheerful winter but winter meant hard times for the unemployed who had been the victims of a trade slump over which they had no control. Every person, then, should try to find some work for these people.

How was this to be done? Rotary and Toc H urged that an appeal be made in every church and Sunday school and at every public or private meeting where speeches were made. Churches were urged to look to their inside or outside painting and renovating at once, and not leave it.

One person might be able to spend £1, another £100. Something could be done in the home perhaps, or in the garden, a garage might be built or repairs done to the car. The appeal concluded by offering no fewer than 101 ideas for jobs to help the victims of the Depression. With the slogan 'Do that job now—don't delay', were listed such items as: paint outside of house, railings, etc.; concrete floor in garage; new garden path in gravel or asphalt; install wireless, carry wireless extensions to other rooms including bedroom; clean or re-press suits, overcoats, etc.; renovate umbrella; new brushes, buckets, and hardware for office; and cleanse factories.

Radios became popular in the 1930s. This model cost about a month's wages.

WITH THE NEW   REVOLUTIONARY 6-PIN VALVES

DESIGNED by the World's Greatest Radio Laboratories . . .

1933 Super-heterodyne

ALL-ELECTRIC RADIO

By

ASTOR

£23/10/

Imposing Cabinet of unusual elegance in polished Walnut and Ebony.
PRICE ONLY . . . .

Judge their superiority yourself.

The essential time to find work was between July and the end of October because this would benefit the unemployed far more than after that date, when it was thought that some of the men would be able to return to their usual trades.

At this time the basic unemployment rate was 7s. 6d. worth of rations a week. Those on the dole were permitted, in addition to sustenance, to earn the value of their rent together with no more than 10s. a week for a man with four or more children.

Single unemployed women not living with parents were generally ignored, although some assistance was available in winter. Their plight during the Depression was particularly bad.

One of the degrading features of the Depression, in the case of people forced to seek assistance, was the attitude of some of the authorities. They sometimes gave the impression they were more concerned with making sure one allegedly undeserving person was detected than ten deserving helped.

In 1934, for instance, applicants could be refused relief for owning even a wireless set. The humiliation of actually listing one's few meagre possessions, or guiltily not giving information about some treasured item which the owner had no intention of selling, can be imagined.

Various public works were undertaken. Perhaps the most famous was the road to the top of Mount Wellington from The Springs. Work was also found in reafforestation. Stories abound of more useless work, such as allegedly digging holes and then having other men fill them in again.

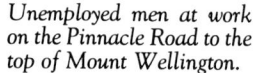

Unemployed men at work on the Pinnacle Road to the top of Mount Wellington.

Victims

The women and children of that decade, if they were not in a family that retained at least one bread-winner, suffered the most.

People could not always afford medical or dental attention, for their children or for themselves, unless it was absolutely necessary, although some doctors accepted payment in other than money or forgot about the bill. Housewives, especially in the cities, were obliged to scratch and scrape to make ends meet. A pound of mince could be made to go a long way, and rabbits (underground mutton) were a godsend as cheap food. Women made do with second-hand dresses and sometimes were ashamed to go out, so poorly dressed they felt themselves to be.

The expense of a marriage could be distressing if not crippling. Newly-weds might be forced to live in a sleep-out or sub-standard accommodation, thus creating tensions in families where the man of the house already felt he had failed in his primary role because he could not get work.

Stories are told of men going out each day and coming back at night, pretending to be at work but in reality simply hanging about. Some headed for the mainland or 'the other side', as it was comly termed, hoping that work might be found there. In the worst cases, men did not find employment at all until late in the 1930s. Others were in and out of work. The depression caused enormous suffering and demoralization.

Children were sometimes forced to leave school, either because they could now get jobs at the junior rate where their elder brothers or sisters, or parents, could not, or because some of the middle classes could no longer afford to pay school fees. Men who had occupied clerical positions found it particularly difficult to cope when put on hard physical work such as road-building.

The bitter feeling that a whole generation had been cheated remained with some of that generation for the rest of their lives. They were the ones who later urged their children to secure government jobs in the belief that they at least would be safe if 'it' happened again. Some people were convinced that the Depression was caused by the banks and would never again put their money in, hoarding it instead. Others developed habits of frugality verging on meanness, or were so shaken by the Depression that they would never risk going into business or taking a chance ever again, always urging caution on their children.

However, some people managed to do quite well out of the Depression. The fact that wages dropped less than prices meant that a person who was able to remain in continual employment at their trade or occupation was actually better off than in the 1920s. Such a person, however, needed to be in constant employment and not be forced to accommodate or finance other family members.

Because rents and payments frequently could not be met, houses came on the market and could be bought cheaply. Some took advantage of this great opportunity and made substantial profits in due course. Some people were evicted from those houses when they could not keep up rental payments and were forced by the landlord to make way for someone who could. A sort of chain reaction resulted: rather than have houses empty and in danger of being vandalized, owners were happy to accept, say, £1 a week rather than £1.10s. simply to have a property occupied. So it went down the line, but at the end there were people who could not afford even very small rentals, or who fell hopelessly behind with payments.

It was these people who were compelled to live with relatives or to occupy makeshift and sub-standard dwellings, shanties or rooms that should have been condemned as unfit for human habitation.

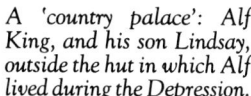

A 'country palace': Alf King, and his son Lindsay, outside the hut in which Alf lived during the Depression.

Children whose parents could afford it sent their offspring to school with two lots of sandwiches during those days, the second one to be pooled and made available to those in the class who had nothing, or very little to eat.

Teachers and the clergy were two groups who saw the effects of the Depression close up. The clergy were always considered likely to give a handout or a small job, such as cutting wood, to a victim who came to the back door (it was always the back door). Every day teachers saw the effects of the Depression on children, heard accounts of how their parents were getting on, and tried to drop a word or hint for help in the right quarter with the local council or charity organization. Many people of course were angry at being thought unable to help themselves. Pride forced some into tragic situations where they simply refused to accept help and desperately kept up appearances as best they could.

Soup kitchens were opened by organizations such as the Salvation Army and people queued for meagre help in a land that had long been considered the working man's paradise. As late as 1938, at a time when the Depression was nearly over, the Salvation Army soup kitchen in Hobart was still supplying soup and bread each day to 150 families and 1500 children.

During the Depression of the 1930s, women and children of Hobart queued with billy cans at a community soup kitchen conducted by the Salvation Army.

One of the worst effects of the Depression was the damage done to the independence and self-reliance of Tasmanians. Some people, it would seem, were able to triumph over adversity, or gave the appearance of doing so. Others, however, were unable to stand the years of degradation and humiliation and the inability to get decent work no matter how hard they tried.

It was always the most degrading of experiences to beg, or pretend to offer something for sale, such as model birds made out of pine cones, or clothes pegs or some other such little objects, unless you had done it often before. No one believed the pitiful facade that the person offering such things was a genuine door-to-door salesman.

Yet Tasmanians, like their fellow Australians, always seemed to blame themselves for their difficulties; the governments, policies and assumptions that had landed the country in the mess it was in were not seriously questioned.

As usual in great social crises, the best and the worst emerged in people—great comradeship and neighbourly feeling on the one hand, calculated exploitation and vicious competition for work on the other.

The birth-rate dropped considerably during the Depression years. This was partly due to fewer couples getting married because they could not afford it, partly to couples refraining from having children at all, for the same reason or because their cramped accommodation made it unthinkable.

In such circumstances, the realization of pregnancy could be a tragedy. Some simply went ahead and had the inconvenient baby, and made the best of it, while others sought advice about birth control (which certain doctors refused to give them on religious grounds). Measures such as abortion (which was illegal and extremely dangerous if performed by an unqualified person) and even sometimes infanticide, were also resorted to.

The incidence of suicide increased during the period of the 1930s. It is not clear whether the figures for theft or prostitution increased significantly or not. It was said that some girls and women were reduced to selling their bodies but the evidence is very difficult to come by. Certainly unemployment and poverty would have made women far more vulnerable to sexual pressures or coercion.

Although it was not much consolation to the cold and hungry, new technology was being introduced all the time. In 1929 automatic telephones made their appearance in Hobart, in 1933 a bi-weekly air service to Melbourne was inaugurated and in 1936 Tasmania was linked to Victoria by submarine phone cable.

By 1938 the first hydro-electric turbines were turning at Tarraleah. The relief work associated with this played some part in helping to alleviate unemployment and the 'Hydro' therefore has pleasant associations for many people who lived through the Depression.

Signs of War

Those Tasmanians who kept up with world affairs were not encouraged by events abroad during the 1930s. Adolf Hitler and the Nazi party came to power in Germany and swept away democratic government, making that country an outlaw nation. Japan invaded Manchuria and began the occupation of China, and the League of

Nations proved unable to stop Italy's venture into Abyssinia (now Ethiopia).

Then in 1936 the Spanish Civil War erupted, renewing a certain amount of religious and political antagonism among Australians, some Catholic spokesmen supporting General Franco and opposing the Republican forces as godless and communistic.

Most Tasmanians, however, were far too preoccupied with their day-to-day existence to worry much about events occurring thousands of miles away over which they had no control.

Hitler's determination to bring all German-speaking peoples under one Reich was accompanied by a policy of racism and the idea of an Aryan 'master race'. The implications of this were first sensed in Tasmania by people of Jewish origin as the Nazi government grew bolder and more anti-Semitic in the course of the decade. Many Tasmanians, however, were slow to believe that the German government could possibly launch attacks on German-Jews who had lived in Germany for generations and who regarded themselves as staunch and loyal German citizens.

In Canberra the Lyons government did little about the impending war except faithfully follow the lead of Britain. Haunted by the ghastly slaughter that had occurred in the trenches of France during the Great War, people understandably felt that any form of arrangement with Hitler which might prevent a repetition of the events of 1914–18 was preferable to a declaration of war.

R. G. Menzies, a rising star in the Australian government, returned from Europe with some positive things to say about Hitler, whom he perceived as having defeated the Depression and given the German people new heart. In actual fact it was the threat of war which did a good deal to alleviate the Depression because a policy of rearmament and spending began. By 1938 unemployment was being substantially reduced and industry encouraged.

At Easter 1939 Tasmanians in particular were stricken to hear that Mr Lyons had died of a heart attack. His body was returned to his native shore and the late prime minister buried at Devonport. The strain of leading Australia during the bleak 1930s took its toll, and it is doubtful if he ever relished the position of prime minister. He once confided that he wished he had never left Tasmania.

The 1930s was a miserable decade for Tasmania and it seemed that nothing could go right when in 1937 an outbreak of infantile paralysis swept the state, crippling some people and leading to the death of others. For many years After Care hospitals reminded Tasmanians that there were attacks even more tragic and insidious than the Depression.

The framework of the state's industry survived intact and the secondary or manufacturing sector may even have been strengthened by hard times. The establishment of pulp and paper mills at Boyer and Burnie at the end of the decade were encouraging signs.

Sport continued, its enjoyment sharpened by the Depression conditions and the prospect of winning a few pounds at cycle or pedestrian events held at carnivals during the Christmas–New Year period (especially along the north-west coast). Sporting heroes such as Don Bradman enjoyed immense popularity and Tasmanians were as enraged as other Australians at the bodyline cricket tour in 1932–3. Phar Lap, the champion race-horse, perhaps best summed up the people's admiration for the battler who came to characterize the Depression, while aviators such as Bert Hinkler and Amy Johnson exemplified what people saw as triumph over adversity in a grim period.

Questions for discussion

1 How and at what point did people qualify for unemployment relief such as the dole and sustenance payments?

2 Who gained and who lost in the Depression in Tasmania?

3 What were the main differences between urban and rural experience of the Depression?

4 Compile a questionnaire to be used in interviewing people who lived through the Depression years. What questions should you ask and not ask? Why? What are the advantages and disadvantages of oral evidence?

Note: For all the above questions, students are advised to talk with people who recall the period.

CHAPTER 8

The 'Good War' ... and After

ON THE EVENING OF SUNDAY, 3 September 1939, only twenty-one years after the end of what was said to be the war to end all wars, Tasmanian people tuned in their wirelesses to hear the new prime minister, R. G. Menzies, announce that because Britain was at war with Germany, then so was Australia.

Nation Informed By Prime Minister

GERMAN PERSISTENCE

MELBOURNE, September 3.

"It is my melancholy duty to inform you officially that in consequence of the persistence by Germany in her invasion of Poland, Great Britain has declared war upon her, and that as a result Australia is also at war," said the Prime Minister (Mr. R. G. Menzies, K.C.) in a broadcast to the Australian people last night.

"No harder task can fall to the lot of a democratic leader than to make such an announcement. Great Britain and France, with the co-operation of the British Dominions, have struggled to avoid this tragedy. They have, as I firmly believe, been patient."

The Distant War

War precautions were at once put into effect and guards placed at ports and aerodromes. Arrangements were made to receive men for enlistment in the Second Australian Imperial Force (AIF), the Royal Australian Air Force (RAAF), and the Royal Australian Navy (RAN). Within a short time, Australian infantry divisions were on their way to North Africa. Shortly after, other units were sent to the great British naval and air base at Singapore, it being feared that the Japanese might strike south.

Once Poland had been defeated by the German forces there was a lull in military activity in Europe. In Australia some petrol rationing was introduced, but for a time day-to-day life was not much affected and people could still feel some sense of detachment from the war. In mid-1940, however, Germany stormed into the Low Countries, Denmark and Norway. Italy declared war against Britain and France.

The allies experienced repeated defeats and with the capitulation of France and the evacuation of the shattered British army from the beaches of Dunkirk, Britain stood alone against the world's mightiest fighting forces.

Tasmanians could only hope for the best as the Luftwaffe unleashed its attacks on what many still fondly called 'Home' or the 'Old Country'. Newsreels and radio broadcasts brought accounts of the death being rained from the sky on British cities. The words 'blitz' and 'London can take it' entered the language and it appeared only a matter of time before Hitler would invade Britain.

It soon became apparent, however, that the RAF was successfully preventing Germany from gaining control of the skies over the English Channel and southern England. The Battle of Britain proved to be a turning point in the war.

The voice of Winston Churchill called upon the people of Britain, the Commonwealth of Nations and the Empire to resist the enemy to the last, to fight on the beaches, in the fields and in the streets and never to surrender.

Far away, Tasmanians took heart from Churchill's voice of defiance and also from news of the defeats inflicted on the Italians in North Africa. Letters from Tasmanian soldiers serving in the area with their accounts of exotic and strange places brought the war closer to home.

Soon things took a different turn. Australian forces were among those sent to Greece and defeated by the advancing German forces. Thrown back into the sea, many were taken to Crete where, again, the Germans triumphed. Letters from some Tasmanian soldiers suddenly ceased: they had been taken prisoner.

The war came closer with the loss of HMAS *Sydney*, with all hands, off the West Australian coast on 19 November 1941, sunk by a German vessel. In Hobart, a 'New *Sydney*' fund was promptly launched to raise money to build a replacement.

Maps of the war zones appeared in many Tasmanian homes. Veterans of the Great War sought to explain as best they could what they perceived to be happening. This war, however, involved incredible mobility in comparison to the trench warfare of 1914–18. The aeroplane and the tank were perfected as new weapons of destruction, employed on a titanic scale.

As islanders, Tasmanians were particularly aware of the importance of sea defence.

(opposite)

In June 1941 Hitler turned his attention east, away from Britain, and plunged into Russia with Operation Barbarossa. Names of Russian towns, cities and regions appeared in Tasmanian newspapers as the Germans smashed across eastern Russia towards

Moscow, only to be halted at the gates of the Soviet capital by stiffening and fanatical resistance by the Red Army and the people, apparently unlimited man- and womanpower, equipment sent by the West and, perhaps most important of all, the Russian winter. The Germans had not prepared for these sub-zero temperatures and appalling weather conditions. The Eastern Front was the graveyard of Hitler's ambitions.

The Pacific War

The war in Europe was the distant war, but on 7 December 1941 came the alarming news that Japanese planes taking off from aircraft carriers had attacked and nearly wiped out the United States base at Pearl Harbor in the Hawaiian Islands, and destroyed many ships and aircraft.

Simultaneously the Japanese launched an attack on Hong Kong and Malaya. Battle-hardened from their campaigns in China, the Imperial Japanese Army pressed south along the Malayan Peninsula, outflanking and out-fighting units that included the 8th Australian Division.

In early 1942 the British battleships *Prince of Wales* and *Repulse* were sunk by attacking Japanese torpedo-carrying aeroplanes. Singapore was captured, together with thousands of Australian servicemen and tens of thousands of Imperial troops in the service of Britain. Tasmanians of the 2/40 Battalion were also taken prisoner in the Dutch East Indies (now Indonesia).

This was a stunning shock to Australia. British power and prestige, which had been taken for granted since the foundation of Australia, was seen to be fallible. 'Impregnable' Singapore was gone. Australia stood alone and defenceless.

The Japanese sliced through the islands north of Australia with frightening ease. On 19 February 1942 Tasmanians knew that the war was coming closer when Darwin was bombed in the largest Japanese air attack since Pearl Harbor. Rumours abounded of Japanese plans to invade Australia after raiding the capital cities from aircraft carriers.

Almost wholly dependent on sea transport, Tasmanians knew that it was very likely that mines would be laid to blow up shipping and that the long-dreaded appearance of modern enemy battleships in the Derwent could not be resisted by puny land gun batteries. Already in 1941 Bass Strait had been closed to shipping because of enemy action, and shortages were experienced in north-west coast towns.

1942 was a crisis year for Australians, as the Japanese advanced along the Kokoda Track over the Owen Stanley Ranges in New Guinea. In this rugged terrain where tropical diseases, the climatic conditions and supply problems hampered all infantry forces, the Japanese got perilously close to Port Moresby, as they pushed the Australian forces back.

Then the tide began to turn. In June 1942 a Japanese naval force heading for Port Moresby was checked by the United States naval and air forces in the Battle of the Coral Sea. At Midway, to the north, the Japanese navy was decisively defeated by the Americans, who had broken the Japanese naval code and so were able to anticipate their movements.

In August, when the enemy attempted a landing at Milne Bay in Papua, Australian forces inflicted the first land defeat of the war on the Japanese. This was an enormous boost to morale.

In New Guinea the Japanese infantry forces began to withdraw, and during the remainder of 1942 were pursued back over the Owen Stanley Ranges to bridgehead positions at Buna and Gona on the coast. Savage battles were waged, with United States forces sending more and more troops, planes and ships to aid the Australians.

In the following years of the war, a large part of the Australian land forces remained in New Guinea, while the Americans under General MacArthur attacked enemy-held islands in the south-west Pacific.

A good deal of criticism of this tactic came to be heard because it was claimed that the Australians, expert jungle fighters as they now were, had been left behind fighting an unnecessary war. Why not simply forget the Japanese in New Guinea and let them starve? The reason seems to lie partly in General MacArthur's ambition to return in triumph to the Philippines and his influence on the Australian government.

Australian forces began to be released from the army for work at home. Germany finally surrendered, and in early August 1945 news came that a strange new weapon had been used to bring the Japanese to their knees.

This was the atomic bomb, dropped on Hiroshima, and then Nagasaki, with devastating effect. Quickly the Japanese surrendered, greatly influenced in their decision by the Russians turning on them. In Tasmania, as elsewhere throughout the Allied nations, there was excited celebration.

The Tasmanian Home Front

In early 1942 Australia was placed on a footing of 'total war'. This meant that all activities had to be measured in terms of their contribution to the war effort. The federal government took control over virtually all aspects of daily life as government regulations laid down what was or was not permissible. Manpower regulations directed the lives of all adults and few doubted the gravity of the situation in which Australia found itself, braced for what was thought to be the inevitable invasion from the Japanese.

In that crisis time, evacuation routes for the civil population were marked out and air raid shelters constructed. The Electrolytic Zinc Company and Cadbury had shelters said to be within one minute's sprinting distance of the exits. All schools practised air raid drills, which involved filing out of classrooms, without panic, into the shelters in preparation for the real thing when the sirens would sound, indicating that hostile aircraft were approaching.

Hobart High School students dug slit trenches on the Domain; the bags on their heads were for camouflage. The Premier (Mr Cosgrove) and the Headmaster (Mr H. V. Biggins) inspected progress.

These trench shelters were usually dug in a zig-zag pattern to prevent the deaths which could have been caused by planes raking along the length of the shelter with machine-gun fire.

Silhouette illustrations of enemy aircraft were issued so that people could recognize a hostile plane. Air Raid Precautions (ARP) involved putting up blackout curtains (usually heavy brown cardboard), masking car headlights and generally following the directions set out in publications and issued by air raid wardens.

Here detailed instructions are given about what to do if the sirens signal the approach of hostile aircraft.

(opposite)

KEEP THIS IN A PROMINENT PLACE FOR REFERENCE.

 CIVIL DEFENCE LEGION: GOVERNMENT OF TASMANIA.

AIR RAID PRECAUTIONS: INSTRUCTIONS TO THE PUBLIC.

The Civil Defence Legion ("C.D.L.") has been established under the authority of the Government of Tasmania for the purpose of safeguarding the civil population in the event of Air Raids. These instructions are issued for the guidance of the public.

You should know that—

1. *The Air Raid Precautions Organisation established by the Civil Defence Legion is available for your assistance in the event of an Air Raid.* You should make yourself acquainted with the arrangements which have been made in your district, and ascertain the names of your Air Raid Warden and his Assistants, and other C.D.L. Officers. You must obey their orders in an emergency, when they will wear official armbands.

2. The chief purpose of Air Raids on Civilian Centres is to cause Panic: Therefore KEEP COOL.

3. In the Event of an Air Raid the Public will be warned by the AIR RAID WARNING SIGNAL. *This consists of a Succession of Intermittent Blasts of about Five Seconds Duration, separated by a Silent Period of about Three Seconds, for a total period of Two Minutes. These Blasts will be sounded on Factory and Railway Whistles and Sirens in various parts of the City or Town. When the Raid is over there will be a Continuous Signal for Two Minutes at a steady pitch.*

4. WHEN THE AIR RAID WARNING IS SOUNDED—

    (*a*) IF AT HOME, STAY THERE, and either remain inside the House or go into the Garden and lie down. If you remain inside the House, lie down as far as possible from the Windows. Turn off Gas at the Meter.

    (*b*) IF AT WORK IN A STEEL OR CONCRETE BUILDING, STAY THERE, preferably on the Ground Floor, and keep away from Windows. IF AT WORK IN ANY OTHER KIND OF BUILDING, GO QUIETLY to the nearest Park, Garden, or Yard, and lie down.

    (*c*) IF IN A CAR, stop the Car, park close to the Side of the Road, and (if at night) turn off the lights. Take cover quietly in the nearest Park, Garden, or Yard, and lie down there.

    (*d*) IF IN A TRAM CAR, leave the Vehicle as quietly as possible, take cover in the nearest Park, Garden, or Yard, and lie down there.

    (*e*) IF IN THE STREET, proceed quietly to the nearest Park, Garden, or Yard, and lie down there. DO NOT RUN.

5. If, during a Raid, you will cover your ears with your hands, the effects of concussion will be reduced.

6. If an Air Raid Warning is sounded at night, *extinguish all lights.*

7. *In the event of Injury or Damage or Fire, report this at once to the nearest Special Constable or other C.D.L. Officer in your District.* He will be wearing an armband. He will summon the necessary assistance. *Do not use the Telephone.* In an emergency the Lines will all be urgently needed for official purposes.

The above instructions contain some essential points for your guidance in an emergency. If it ever becomes necessary, you will be given further advice and information as to what to do. If you are uncertain on any point, consult your Air Raid Warden, who will gladly give you all assistance possible.

Remember above all—Don't give way to panic: take it quietly, and obey instructions.

G. A. WALCH,
Director of Civil Defence.
August, 1940.

T. H. DAVIES,
Minister for Lands and Works and
Minister in Charge of Civil Defence Legion.

Air raid shelter, Franklin Square, Hobart. Sand bags were thought to be most effective against bullets or bomb blast.

Pamphlets were issued about how to put out incendiary bombs and how to seek protection from high explosive bombs. Casualty stations were prepared for the victims of potential bombing raids.

Censorship was imposed on newspapers so the government could inform the population of what it thought they should know and keep out news items that it was thought might be of value to the enemy. People were urged to keep quiet about what they knew or had been told of troop movements or anything to do with defence. Australian posters based on those produced in England warned that idle chatter might cost lives. Hatred of the Japanese was encouraged by the issue of posters warning that the enemy was coming south.

All this was a trifle unreal in Tasmania. The state was undoubtedly further away from the land fighting than anywhere in Australia and, after the crisis months of early 1942, it became clear that the enemy was scarcely likely to launch an invasion of the mainland by first bombing and then occupying the island state.

In April 1942 the people were heartened by the arrival in Australia of General Douglas MacArthur who took control of Allied Land Forces, South-West Pacific Area. Ever-increasing numbers of American troops arrived and the AIF forces recalled from North Africa by the Australian prime minister, John Curtin, also strengthened the civilian population's morale.

In comparison with Melbourne and Brisbane, Tasmania saw little of the Americans, apart from those men who were crew on American vessels such as the Liberty ships.

The dangers of careless talk were first stressed in Britain; the Australian government adapted the same idea to the Japanese threat overshadowing the nation.

Tasmanian families had sons, husbands and brothers at the war in three main theatres of operation: as airmen in North Africa and Britain; soldiers in North Africa with the Sixth, Seventh and Ninth divisions; and, increasingly, in New Guinea, Papua and the adjacent islands, with both the AIF and the non-volunteer Militia. Naval men were scattered across the seven seas.

Conscription to the armed forces was not introduced until late 1942. Until then, enlistment was voluntary (during the Great War conscription had been a catastrophically divisive issue).

WHAT'S **YOUR** EXCUSE FOR NOT JOINING YOUR COMRADES IN THE *AIF* ?

GET SQUARE WITH YOUR CONSCIENCE - ENLIST NOW

Many Tasmanian service personnel, however, had been captured. Those taken prisoner by the Japanese included seven doctors and three nurses. Those shot down in North African areas or over western Europe were taken by the Germans.

Sporadic word came from Japanese radio messages said to come from captives. There were sinister signs that not all was well. A rumour had it that a message received from à Launceston soldier said he was being well-treated but wished he was in Carr Villa with his father—Carr Villa was the site of a cemetery in which his father was buried.

The full story of how Australians fared at the hands of the Japanese did not emerge during the war. It was only after the surviving POWs were released and had returned home that horrified Tasmanians learnt of the losses and of the experiences suffered in the camps.

Yet in a curious way, the war of 1939–45 was a 'good war' for many people on the home front in Tasmania. Some 2000 women found a sense of service and duty in joining the various Auxiliary Forces attached to the three main fighting services. Many others were in the Women's Land Army, the Voluntary Aid Detachment, the Red Cross, the Australian Comforts Fund and related organizations. Others worked in factories turning out war material. All earned money, more than some had ever had before, and all felt they were doing their bit for the war effort. There was a great sense of community effort in this, something that had been partially lacking during the Great War.

The Australian Women's Land Army was officially established in July 1942. There had earlier been privately-sponsored land army women, as here in January 1942.

(left)

Woman-power solidly behind Tasmania's war production effort, making socks in a factory.

(right)

Nor were there the deeply divisive campaigns about conscription which had so scarred Tasmania in 1916 and 1917. The federal Labor government managed to secure an agreement for a form of conscription whereby the militia were able to serve side by side with AIF volunteers in a loosely-defined area north of New Guinea. Labor was in power at the federal level from late 1941, and in Tasmania throughout the entire course of the war. There was a sense of great coherence and shared purpose in Australia, particularly during 1942–3.

War activity in Tasmania took many forms. A Volunteer Defence Corps was created from more than 4000 men debarred from enlisting because they were too old or in reserved occupations. They were employed in coastal defence, coast watching and anti-aircraft and searchlight services. Many were veterans of the Great War and trained themselves afresh, thinking of the guerrilla tactics possible to resist an enemy landing and occupation of the state.

ARP services had 14 000 volunteers, with chief air raid wardens in all urban centres. Special police were sworn in. Aid posts, emergency hospitals and depots were established and training given in rescue demolition work, gas decontamination, transport and canteen services.

Some youths from sixteen to eighteen years joined the Air Training Corps from 1941. Of 676 enrolled and given part-time instruction, 156 were admitted to the RAAF as air-crew, one of them later winning the Distinguished Flying Cross for service in the RAAF and the RAF. A Naval Auxiliary Patrol was also organized to supplement the work of the fighting navy and numerous wooden ships were built by the experienced shipwrights at the Hobart yards.

Campaigns were organized to collect metal such as aluminium kitchen ware for use in aircraft production or waste paper for recycling. Camouflage nets were made.

Collection of aluminium was said to aid the war effort and certainly boosted morale.

People were urged to invest their surplus money in War Loans and War Savings Certificates. Streets were designated 'War Savings' streets, to show how the people were aiding the war effort financially. Money poured in from the earnings of those who had been scratching for a shilling during the Depression only a few years earlier. Full employment, price control and reduced spending opportunities meant there was a lot of money about. Although goods were in short supply it was somehow usually possible to purchase these items through black marketeers. Silk stockings disappeared from the scene but some women resourcefully used eyebrow pencil or something similar to mark in seams. Inflation and prices were kept under control by strong federal legislation and people were issued with identification cards and official ration books of coupons to limit purchases of food, clothing and petrol.

Ration books were issued during the war to help control the economy and to ensure equality of sacrifice.

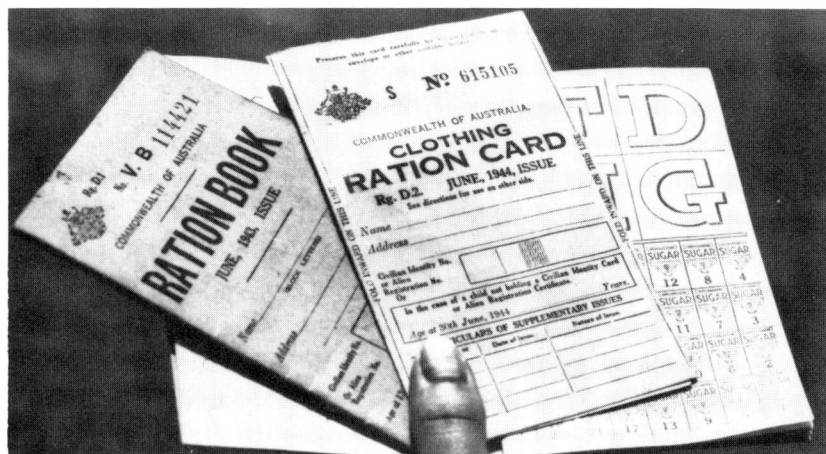

In June 1942 the Pacific War was at crisis point. Here the Premier and Mrs Cosgrove received their ration books.

Tasmanians during the war of 1939–45 suffered minimally on the home front in comparison with the inhabitants of the British Isles. In relation to many of the people in Europe and especially the Soviet Union and enemy-occupied countries, they had very little experience of war at all.

At the beginning of the war, suspected or enemy aliens were rounded up and interned or kept under observation by the police. Some of these people were Italians who had been in Australia for years. By degrees they were restored to their families and businesses, some extremely annoyed because their connection with Italy was very slight or their attachment to the Fascist regime of Mussolini non-existent or antagonistic.

Another quite different group of Italians were the soldiers captured in North Africa. Tasmania, founded as a jail, was a hard place to escape from and took quite a number of Italian prisoners of war.

Generally the Italians were well-treated because people liked to think—or hope—that Tasmanian POWs were being treated in the same way. The Italians' main problem appears to have been loneliness. Importantly, the Italians represented a form of cheap labour at a time when farm workers were in very short supply. Some later returned to Tasmania, migrants with a difference.

Growth of Industry and Agriculture

Tasmania's isolation, its small population and relatively low level of industrialization meant that few war factories or large businesses were sited in the state at the beginning of the war. Workers soon began to leave Tasmania, attracted by the opportunities on offer in Victoria. Alarmed at this trend, the Tasmanian government made numerous efforts to attract war-related industry to the state. They met with some success and, by December 1943, 1350 workers, including 850 women, were employed at an ammunition factory at Derwent Park, near Hobart, making such items as mortar bomb cases.

The Launceston railway workshops were responsible for producing enormous amounts of essential war equipment such as bridging, landing barges, machine tools and gauges, and so on. These workshops also produced 25-pounder shells and 4.2 in. mortar bombs.

Launceston foundries played a particularly important part in Tasmania's contribution to the war effort. The Salisbury Foundry turned out the largest single casting ever produced in the state, as well as such items as propellors. The Phoenix Foundry constructed steam winches and cranes. The Glasgow Engineering Company and Reconditioned Motors Pty Ltd also turned out war equipment under government contracts. Similarly, textile and clothing works in Launceston boomed under the effect of war orders.

Wolfram and scheelite production was increased at Storey's Creek, Aberfoyle and King Island because the Japanese had occupied the areas from which these substances had earlier been imported. Henry Jones and Company went over to war production of bolts, nuts and primers for shells. The firm also produced a million gallons of apple juice and millions of tins of preserved fruit and jams.

An interesting consequence of the war was the establishment of the Waterworth Optical Annexe at the rear of the University of Tasmania, then on the old Domain site. Starting virtually from scratch, scientists and technicians began producing prisms for gun artillery sights, which were then in very short supply in Australia. This was work of the utmost importance to the Australian war effort. It called for great intelligence and skill and within a year some two hundred men and women were engaged in the intricate task.

The federal government played a major part in the rapid growth of essential and war-related industries in Tasmania. An essential factor behind the rapid growth was Canberra's ability to co-ordinate the war effort and production of war supplies. To help achieve the necessary centralization, the federal Labor government passed legislation of the highest importance. In 1942 the Uniform Taxation Act was passed which gave into the hands of the central government the taxing powers previously held by the states.

No other measure was as important as this in weakening the power of the state governments and bringing about a national feeling over and above a state one. It had taken the grave emergency of war and the threat of invasion and bloodshed on Australian soil to accomplish it. The legislation was agreed to in the spirit of Mr Curtin's inspired call to the Australian people to fight together as they had never fought before and work together as they had never worked before.

The war led to a great demand for aluminium. Being a light metal, it was particularly suitable for aircraft production and so in April 1941 the Australian government decided to establish an aluminium smelter. Tasmania was chosen because there was cheap electric power and, possibly, because it was difficult for any enemy to attack, being isolated and distant from war zones. However, federal and state governments only came to an agreement in 1944 and a factory was begun the next year on the Tamar estuary and production started in 1955.

Fifteen years later this industry, which owed its existence directly to the war, employed about 1000 people and used about a quarter of the hydro-electricity generated in the state. The raw material was bauxite, shipped by bulk carriers to Bell Bay from Weipa on the Cape York Peninsula.

Similarly the war led to urgent demand for zinc alloy castings with a very high level of purity, from the Electrolytic Zinc Company. Cadmium, mercury, cobalt oxide, sulphuric acid, superphosphate, sulphate of ammonia and aluminium sulphate were other products. In 1964 the Company bought the North Mount Farrell mines at Tullah and very high-grade silver-lead ore was extracted.

Another company whose fortunes were linked to the war and its aftermath was the Goliath Portland Cement Company. Owned predominantly by Tasmanian shareholders, unlike the other large industries established in the state, this company had an annual capacity of 100 000 tons by the outbreak of the war, doubling by 1956 at which time an asbestos-cement factory was in production.

The war had beneficial effects on a range of Tasmanian industries not necessarily linked to the war effort. In 1938 Australian Newsprint Mills built a factory at Boyer. Three years later the first paper machine started up and the war did no apparent harm to the business. A second such machine became operative in 1951 and a third in 1969, supplying nearly all the newsprint for newspapers throughout Australia.

Similarly the Associated Pulp and Paper Mills commenced operations at Burnie in 1938, producing paper, hardboard, sawn timber and wood pulp. This mill gave most important employment to people from the area both during and after the war. From a population of little more than 7000 in 1947, Burnie doubled its size by 1966, aided by the establishment at Heybridge of Australian Titan Products with its paint pigment factory.

Primary production too was given an enormous boost by the 'good war'. For example, in 1939–40, Tasmanian production of apple sauce and dried apples was negligible, despite the excellent conditions for apple-growing. By 1943–4 this situation had changed in an extraordinary way due to war demand, and Tasmania produced no fewer than 10 million pounds weight of apple sauce and 4.3 million pounds weight of dried apples.

North-west agricultural areas especially had a 'good war'. Potato crops rocketed from 30 000 acres to 90 000 acres under the contract system enforced by the government. The average yearly sowing of blue peas was 8500 acres before the war, but by 1944 was no less than 38 000 acres.

In 1942 three vegetable dehydration factories were put in hand by the federal government as part of the war effort. They were code-named Dewcrisp (Scottsdale), Dewpearl (Ulverstone) and Dewpoint (Smithton). Then in 1944 a vegetable canning factory was established at Devonport. It was operated with the assistance of the American giant H. J. Heinz. During the war, production of canned vegetables rose from 600 000 pounds weight to 2.5 million, representing about 90 per cent of the entire Australian production.

Potato dehydration factory at Ulverstone during the war.

Later the factories at Devonport and Ulverstone were bought by Edgells, and given over to the production of frozen, dried and canned products, grown readily on the fertile soils of the north-west. The Edgell Division of Petersville, and its distribution network, enabled many primary producers in the area to look back on the 'good war' as the time when they got on their feet, economically speaking.

In the last season before the war, 59 per cent of Tasmania's apple crop was exported overseas and 34 per cent interstate. However, nearly all the interstate trade was lost after the war because of increased production in the mainland states coupled with high freight charges.

The overseas market was retained, and in 1961–2 the value of fresh apple exports sent abroad accounted for nearly 25 per cent of the state's overseas export earnings. In this case, however, the war was not 'good' for the state since the conflict in Europe was a prime factor leading to the creation of the European Economic Community which, it was hoped, would prevent any more disasters such as the wars of 1914–18 and 1939–45. With Britain's entry into the EEC, the once-famous Tasmanian apple industry was in deep trouble.

The stimulus to the economy and business given by the war and its results was also apparent in other areas of Tasmanian industry. Before the war, dairy production in the state was characterized as much by its subsistence nature as by scientific and business-like farming, but the war meant that rational, large-scale production was necessary. Culling and grading of dairy herds was encouraged by the Agricultural Department and by the end of the war 30 million gallons of milk were being produced by Tasmanian dairy-farmers.

This rose to 100 million gallons by 1972, about 20 per cent of the total gross value of rural production in the state. After 1960 dairy cans became obsolete and were replaced with refrigerated and stainless steel tankers, with Cadbury buying the product for manufacture of confectionery such as chocolates. By 1972, 70 per cent of milk was converted into butter and 23 per cent into cheese, with the United Kingdom the main outlet.

Twenty years after the end of the 'good war', farming output in the state had doubled and labour input declined by one-third. This was largely due to mechanization made possible by investment of the money made during the war. The war also played an important part in steadying and controlling growth, providing a sound base for continued expansion in later years. By 1953/4 the value of factory production exceeded the value of primary production for the first time.

Clearly, the developments and changes in Tasmania during and since the war of 1939–45 can largely be traced to the impact of that conflict. However, factors such as the growth of national and international businesses, immigration, and the continuing financial power and influence of the federal government also played a part. The large amounts of money saved and invested undoubtedly make the period 1939–45 one which can be termed the 'good war'.

In the 1960s a mining boom began which may be compared with the growth of that industry in the 1890s when Zeehan and Mount Lyell burst upon the scene. Ironically, the defeated enemy of only a few years before played a central part in this. In 1965 Japanese interests concluded a deal concerning production of iron pellets from the Savage River area and their removal to Port Latta for shipping away. The Japanese also became increasingly involved in buying Tasmanian products such as woodchips, and in exploiting the deep-sea fishing in and off Tasmanian waters.

By the 1960s Tasmania was relatively more industrialized than Western Australia or Queensland, with more than one-third of total production centred on Hobart.

Public Works

For the people of Hobart, the most spectacular immediate effect of the war was the sudden bridging of the wide and deep Derwent estuary in 1943. Until then the eastern shore had been quite thinly populated and had connected with the central business district only by ferry.

The new floating bridge consisted of twenty-four curved concrete pontoons spanning about 1000 metres of water and weighing over 24 000 tonnes. The pontoons were floated into position and connected end to end, with provision for barge traffic to the Australian Newsprint Mills upriver and for cargo vessels going to and from the Electrolytic Zinc Company works. This cross-river link, created by the emergency of war, led to large-scale growth in building on the eastern shore. By 1955 road traffic had become congested, with irritating delays when the lift span was elevated to let river traffic through. Finally in 1964 the new Tasman bridge was opened. It was situated downstream from the old bridge and built of a little less than 1000 metres of pre-stressed concrete.

The development of Bell Bay and George Town in relation to the aluminium works originally located in the area because of the war, served to underline the isolation of the coastal north-east region from the north-west. During the economically prosperous times of the 1960s, plans were made to remedy this situation by bridging the Tamar. A new bridge was constructed thirty-eight kilometres downstream from Launceston and ten kilometres upstream from Bell Bay, at Whirlpool Reach where the Tamar contracted to about 220 metres across. The bridge, named after John Batman, one of the Launceston settlers who founded Melbourne, was opened in 1968.

The Tasman Bridge over the Derwent at Hobart.

Population Increase

After the war the Australian government decided upon a policy of extensive immigration from Europe. While part of the reason for this lay in a long-standing feeling that Australia must 'develop' and 'populate or perish', the policy arose as a direct result of the war.

The recent threat in the Pacific was seen as a warning and served to confirm the government's position. In addition there was concern on the part of some groups in Australia about the fate of displaced persons. As a result of the war large numbers of people had been displaced from their home countries and could not return or did not wish to for political reasons. Many could not return because frontiers between east and west had virtually been closed.

Thus it was that under the leadership of the Minister for Immigration, Arthur Calwell, Tasmania began to receive European immigrants from European countries other than Britain. The new postwar generation of schoolchildren began to include boys and girls with surnames previously unknown to the vast majority of Tasmanians. While most of the newcomers still came from Britain and Ireland, as they had always done, Dutch, German and Polish people were also particularly attracted to the state. For the first time in the twentieth century, Tasmania's annual rate of population increase exceeded that of the nation as a whole. Whereas between 1933 and 1947 Australia's population as a whole grew at the rate of 0.96 per cent compared to Tasmania's 0.87 per cent, in the period 1947–54 the Australian figure was 2.46 in comparison to Tasmania's 2.65. Between 1954 and 1961, however, the overall Australian figure was 2.2 per cent compared to 1.82 per cent in the island state.

This pattern persisted. In 1961–6 the figures were 1.88 and 1.18 for Australia as a whole and Tasmania respectively. In 1966–71 the figures were 1.92 and 1.00. From 1976–81 the comparative figures were 1.24 and 0.72 per cent.

Between 1966 and 1971 the population of Hobart and the southern region increased from 174 000 to 183 000. In the same period the population of Launceston and the north rose from 106 000 to 107 000, and that of the north-west and west from 90 000 to 100 000.

Despite the large migrant intake immediately after the war, the state remained relatively untouched by immigration compared with the other states. In 1971, 91 per cent of Tasmania's population was born in Australia, New Zealand or Great Britain. By 1981 it was up to 95 per cent, the other main national groups coming from the Netherlands, Germany, Poland and Italy. Victoria, by comparison, had four times the number of people derived from non-British Europe as did Tasmania.

Questions for discussion

1   How would a person visiting Tasmania from a neutral country in early 1942 have known there was a war on?

2   What happened to Tasmanian service personnel taken prisoner by the Japanese and the Germans, and why?

3   What main effects did the war have on employment and primary and secondary industry in Tasmania?

4   What do you understand by the term 'development' as used in Tasmania, and to what extent is it based in the history of the state?

Note: For all the above questions, students are advised to talk with people who recall the period.

CHAPTER 9

Conclusion

F OR MUCH OF ITS HISTORY, Van Diemen's Land, one of the first-settled colonies of Australia, was isolated, leading to a strong sense of being different. As well, tiny size and population in comparison with the rest of Australia, together with lack of substantial economic development until well into the twentieth century, contributed to the island's feeling of being overlooked and not given enough attention. Becoming something of a backwater, Tasmania historically developed a sensitivity to criticism and a strong sense of provincialism. These characteristics have persisted in the form of a slightly belligerent outlook towards others.

Wrest Point Casino was a controversial development.
(left)

The roll-on roll-off ferry Abel Tasman enormously aided the tourist industry.
(right)

Compared to the position in 1901 or 1939, however, the Tasmania of the late 1980s appears an utterly different place, at least superficially. Motor transport has been enormously facilitated by the road-building programmes of the 1960s. The roll-on roll-off vessels which now cross Bass Strait have generated a revolution in the hospitality and tourism industries.

The work of the National Trust, historians and writers has contributed to an increased interest in historic buildings and landmarks. Their cultural, historic and tourist value and potential, as well as the unique natural beauty and variety of the island's landscape, is now well-understood.

At the same time Tasmania has become Americanized. Supermarket chains, fast food outlets and American television programmes are now much in evidence. In many respects the historically isolated colony and state has been woven into the fabric of Australian and indeed international business.

The success of the federation movement and the crucial taxation legislation of 1942 locked Tasmania ever more firmly into the position of a claimant state, so that a very large proportion of its revenue came to be annually accepted from the federal government.

As one result of being part of the global village, Tasmania experienced the effect of such movements as Black Power and Friends of the Earth. People in Tasmania of Aboriginal origin began making demands and rediscovering their history.

In the 1970s and 1980s the Friends of the Earth and environmental movements gathered strength. Tasmanians found themselves suddenly a focus of world attention when the government sought to flood Lake Pedder to provide more water for hydro-electric power, and to build a dam on the Franklin River. As elsewhere in the western world, conservation groups appeared determined to resist onslaughts on the natural environment. To the annoyance of some, they began asking awkward questions concerning the long-term costs of development.

The Conservation Movement in Tasmania received world-wide attention during the Franklin Dam upheaval.

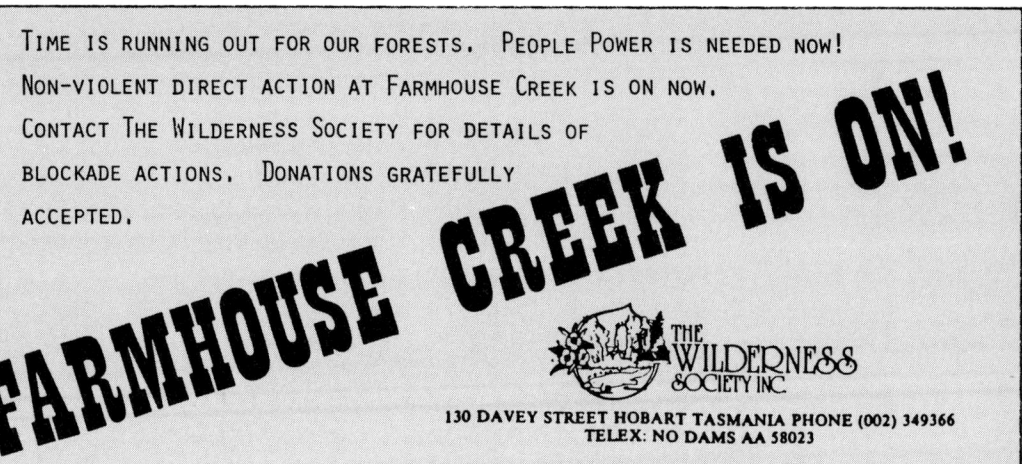

TIME IS RUNNING OUT FOR OUR FORESTS. PEOPLE POWER IS NEEDED NOW!
NON-VIOLENT DIRECT ACTION AT FARMHOUSE CREEK IS ON NOW.
CONTACT THE WILDERNESS SOCIETY FOR DETAILS OF
BLOCKADE ACTIONS. DONATIONS GRATEFULLY
ACCEPTED.

FARMHOUSE CREEK IS ON!

THE WILDERNESS SOCIETY INC.
130 DAVEY STREET HOBART TASMANIA PHONE (002) 349366
TELEX: NO DAMS AA 58023

A leaflet issued by the Wilderness Society in early 1987.

Passions became aroused and the most serious questions arose about the role of the Hydro-Electric Commission and the elected parliament of Tasmania, the rights and duties of the Australian government and the position of the federal law courts.

The hope that had been placed in the Hydro-Electric Commission and the expansion of secondary industry as a means of aiding in the development of Tasmania was called into question. Critics pointed out that increased secondary industry did not automatically imply more employment because computerization and automation were fast taking jobs. Others queried whether it was wise to destroy as much of the natural environment as was planned at a time when tourism seemed to be developing into a multi-million dollar industry.

Clearly a drama was being played out which went to the heart of the state and its people. Questions came to be asked about who actually owned Tasmania, who in the final analysis called the shots, and who really put up the money for the day-to-day administration.

The answers to these and related questions reside in historical analysis of the present situation. We cannot understand what we are doing or will do today, without understanding what happened to us yesterday and why it happened.

How Tasmanians came to be what they are can only be explained by an understanding of the history of Tasmania.

Further Reading

General References

The *Australian Dictionary of Biography* (Melbourne, 1966–present), although it is not yet finished, should be used to look up the principal people mentioned.

Another useful source, if you have access to it, is the *Papers and Proceedings* of the Tasmanian Historical Association (Hobart, 1951–present).

Local histories and studies of Tasmania, found in libraries and bookshops, can provide much interesting material and will be helpful in answering some of the questions at the end of chapters.

Lloyd Robson's *A History of Tasmania*, volume 1 (Melbourne, 1983) and *A Short History of Tasmania* (Melbourne, 1985) can be used to supplement the information in *The Tasmanian Story*, or can be read in association with it. Although volume 1 only covers the period to the 1850s, the second volume, from the 1850s on will be available from 1988.

Another useful general history is John West's *The History of Tasmania* (Launceston, 1852, reprinted 1966, 1971).

1 Invasion

Plomley, N. J. B. *The Tasmanian Aborigines*, Launceston, 1977.
Robson, L. L. *A History of Tasmania*, vol. 1, Melbourne, 1983.
Robson, L. L. *To the Last Breath*, Sydney, 1980.
Ryan, Lyndall. *The Aboriginal Tasmanians*, St Lucia, 1981.

2 The Colony Fully Established

Fitzpatrick, Kathleen. *Sir John Franklin in Tasmania, 1937–43*, Melbourne, 1949.
Plomley, N. J. B. (ed.). *Friendly Mission: The Tasmanian Journals and Papers of George Augustus Robinson 1829–34*, Hobart, 1966.
Robson, L. L. *The Convict Settlers of Australia*, Melbourne, 1965.
Robson, L. L. *A History of Tasmania*, vol. 1, Melbourne, 1983.
Shaw, A. G. L. *Convicts and the Colonies*, London, 1966.
Shaw, A. G. L. *Sir George Arthur, Bart.*, Melbourne, 1980.
Turnbull, Clive. *Black War*, Melbourne, 1948.

3 Tensions and Depression

Reynolds, Henry. ' "That Hated Stain": The Aftermath of Transportation in Tasmania', *Historical Studies*, vol. 14, no. 53, October 1969, pp. 19–31.
Robson, L. L. *A History of Tasmania*, vol. 1, Melbourne, 1983.
Shaw, A. G. L. *Convicts and the Colonies*, London, 1966.

4 Prosperity

Bennett, Scott. *Federation*, Melbourne, 1975.

Blainey, G., 'Population Movements in Tasmania 1870–1901', *Tasmanian Historical Research Association*, Papers and Proceedings, vol. 3, no. 4, 1954, pp. 62–70.

Blainey, G. *The Peaks of Lyell*, Melbourne, 1954.

Blainey, G. 'The Rise and Decline of the West Coast', Tasmanian Historical Research Association, *Papers and Proceedings*, vol. 4, no. 4, February 1956, pp. 66–74.

5 Advances and Reversals

Broinowski, L. (ed.). *Tasmania's War Record 1914–18*, Hobart, 1921.

Davis, Richard. *Eighty Years' Labor: The ALP in Tasmania, 1903–83*, Hobart, 1983.

Lake, Marilyn. *A Divided Society: Tasmania during World War I*, Melbourne, 1975.

Phillips, Derek. *Making More Adequate Provision: State Education in Tasmania, 1839–1985*, Hobart, 1985.

6 The 1920s

Hart, P. R. 'J. A. Lyons, Tasmanian Labor Leader', *Labour History*, no. 9, November 1965, pp. 33–42.

Phillips, Derek. *Making More Adequate Provision: State Education in Tasmania, 1830–1985*, Hobart, 1985.

Reynolds, J. 'The Establishment of the Electrolytic Zinc Company in Tasmania', Tasmanian Historical Research Association, *Papers and Proceedings*, vol. 6, no. 2, September 1957, pp. 26–35.

Robson, L. L. *Australia in the 1920s: Commentary and Documents*, Melbourne, 1980.

7 The Great Depression

Batt, N. 'Tasmania's Depression Elections', *Labour History*, no. 17, 1970, pp. 111–20.

Batt, N. 'Unemployment in Tasmania 1928–33', Tasmanian Historical Research Association, *Papers and Proceedings*, vol. 25, no. 3, September 1978, pp. 46–70.

Spenceley, G. *The Depression Decade*, Melbourne, 1981.

8 The 'Good War' ... and After

Dunlop, E. E. *The War Diaries of Weary Dunlop: Java and the Burma–Thailand Railway 1942–45*, Melbourne, 1986.

O'Brien, Matt. *Tasmania's War Effort*, Launceston, 1946.

Roberts, Barney. *A Kind of Cattle*, Canberra, 1985.

Robertson, John. *Australia Goes to War*, Sydney, 1984.

Acknowledgements

For assistance in collecting the illustrations, special thanks are due to Shirley Eldershaw (Archives Office of Tasmania), Alison Cupit (Tasmanian Museum and Art Gallery), Rhonda Hamilton (Queen Victoria Museum and Art Gallery) and Geoffrey Stilwell (Allport Library and Museum of Fine Arts).

The author and publishers wish to thank copyright holders for supplying and granting permission to reproduce photographs and posters. Sources of illustrations are as follows:

Alison Alexander and Glenorchy City Council, Tasmania, from *Glenorchy 1804–1964* (1986), p. 88; Allport Library and Museum of Fine Arts, State Library of Tasmania, Hobart, pp. 2, 11, 16, 23, 26, 32; Archives Office of Tasmania, Hobart, pp. 40, 42 (top), 44, 47, 50, 52, 61, 65, 68, 100; Australian War Memorial, Canberra, pp. 58, 105 top, 109; W. L. Crowther Library, State Library of Tasmania, Hobart, p. 12; Department of Tourism, Hobart, p. 111; J. W. B. Murphy Collection, State Library of Tasmania, Hobart, p. 55; *Mercury*, Hobart, pp. 86, 89, 93, 98, 103, 104, 105 bottom, 115; *Mercury*, Hobart, and J. J. Cowburn, p. 83; *Mercury*, Hobart, and the Archives Office of Tasmania, Hobart, pp. 74 bottom left, 76, 78, 85, 95; Mitchell Library, State Library of New South Wales, Sydney, p. 25 top left, National Library of Australia, Canberra, pp. 21, 34, 81, Platypus Press, *The Hobart Town Gazette* (1965), vol. I and II (no. 40, 1 March 1817), p. 8; Queen Victoria Museum and Art Gallery, Launceston, pp. 25 bottom right, 30, 74 top; N. Redmond, 'Etablissement Pénitentiaire de Port Arthur', in Laplace, *Circumnavigation de la Frégate L'Artemise*, 1853, p. 18; portrait of Sir George Arthur located by Professor A. G. L. Shaw, p. 13; Collection: Tasmanian Museum and Art Gallery, Hobart, pp. 3, 4, 5, 35, 42 bottom, 51, 75; Tasmaniana Library, State Library of Tasmania, Hobart, pp. 48, 60, 67, 70, 99, 101, 102; Photographs supplied by Tourism Tasmania, Melbourne, p. 114; Courtesy of the Wilderness Society, Hobart, p. 116.

Index